christian. muslim. friend.

Twelve Paths to

Real Relationship

"As the storms of conflict rage between Muslims and Christians, this book is a thunderclap of grace. Without compromising his convictions and coming from deep personal experiences, David Shenk brings powerful wisdom and empathy to a divided world."
— **Rachel Pieh Jones, writer and blogger**

"This book is infused with evidence of the author's personal integrity shaped by a tradition of Christianity known for its unambiguous commitment to peace and peacebuilding. This work will appeal to all Christians seeking to relate to Muslims; it will also connect with Muslims open to seeing a sympathetic reflection of themselves in its pages."
— **David Singh, research tutor in Islamic studies, Oxford Centre for Mission Studies**

"I have not only learned much from this book, but I have also been greatly challenged in the way I seek to build relationships in peacemaking. I heartily recommend this book to all who are keen to build bridges to the Muslim community."
— **Tan Kok Beng, chair, Bethany International University, Singapore**

"Out of a deep well of experience, Shenk provides instructive, practical ways for Christians to journey with Muslims as *friends*. I strongly recommend this book for those who seek to be bearers of God's message of reconciliation in a broken and troubled world."
— **John Azumah, associate professor of w**
 Columbia Theological Seminary

"Shenk insists that we can remain deeply committed to our own faith while pursuing authentic relationship with those deeply committed to theirs. His lifelong experience with Christian-Muslim interaction offers both clarity about the challenges of these relationships and hope for peace among all the children of Abraham."
— **Laurie Mellinger, academic dean, Evangelical Seminary**

"At this critical hour, Shenk's prophetic call to close the chapter of historic mistrust and hostility—and embrace with hope the risk of sincerely conversing with one's Muslim neighbors—must be accepted by all who seek peace in the world."
— **Andrew F. Bush, professor of missions, Eastern University**

"Provides practical steps, thoughtful analysis of competing approaches, and inspiring examples of how to respectfully engage Muslims without compromising a commitment to Christ. This book's message is sorely needed on our college campuses in this age in which relativism and hostility seem to be the only available options."
— **Lorri Bentch, vice president of operations, Christian Union**

"Drawing on his personal experiences in many Muslim countries, Shenk provides deep insights from his Christian faith with humility and transparency. At the same time he names the differences between the two Abrahamic faiths, leaving readers to draw their own conclusions. I heartily endorse this very important book."
— **Nelson Okanya, president, Eastern Mennonite Missions**

"The many stories of direct personal engagement with Muslims from various countries and walks of life demonstrate that real dialogue, where both parties are true to their deepest convictions, is possible. In fact, such dialogue is the only kind worth having. If your deep desire is to love Muslims as Jesus does, this book will be a great aid in walking that path."
— **Steven J. Van Zanen, director for missions education and engagement, Christian Reformed World Missions**

"David Shenk has been a guest in our home during the years our family served in central Asia and often wove entertaining stories for us about his adventures in Africa. This book is no different, combining many personal stories with important lessons about the paths that lead to strong Christian-Muslim relationships."
— **Sara H. Martin, student, Wheaton College**

the CHRISTIANS MEETING MUSLIMS *series*

christian. muslim. friend.

Twelve Paths to
Real Relationship

David W. Shenk

Herald Press

Harrisonburg, Virginia
Kitchener, Ontario

Library of Congress Cataloging-in-Publication Data

Shenk, David W., 1937-, author.
   Christian, Muslim, friend : twelve paths to real relationship / David W.
Shenk.
      pages cm
   Includes bibliographical references.
   ISBN 978-0-8361-9905-5 (pbk. : alk. paper) 1. Islam--Relations--Chris-
tianity. 2. Christianity and other religions--Islam. 3. Peace-building--Reli-
gious aspects--Christianity. 4. Religious pluralism--Christianity. I. Title.
   BP172.S5138 2014
   261.2'7--dc23
                                    2014028458

CHRISTIAN. MUSLIM. FRIEND.
Copyright © 2014 by Herald Press, Harrisonburg, Virginia 22802
   Released simultaneously in Canada by Herald Press,
   Kitchener, Ontario N2G 3R1. All rights reserved.
Library of Congress Control Number: 2014028458
International Standard Book Number: 978-0-8361-9905-5
Printed in the United States of America
Cover and interior design by Reuben Graham

Scriptures taken from the Holy Bible, *New International Version*®, NIV®.
Copyright © 1973, 1978, 1984, 2011 by Biblica, Inc.™ Used by permission of Zondervan. All rights reserved worldwide. www.zondervan.com
The "NIV" and "New International Version" are trademarks registered in
the United States Patent and Trademark Office by Biblica, Inc.™

Qur'an quotations are from The Holy Qur'an, Text, Translation, and
Commentary, by Abdullah Yusuf Ali. Published (1968) under supervision
of Dar al Arabia, Beirut, Lebanon.

To order or request information, please call 1-800-245-7894 in the U.S. or
1-800-631-6535 in Canada. Or visit www.heraldpress.com

18 17 16 15 14   10 9 8 7 6 5 4 3 2 1

To Ahmed Ali Haile,
an ambassador of peace

Contents

Foreword

Many years ago David Shenk and I were in Hartford, Connecticut, going to an evening lecture on Muslim-Christian relations by Kenneth Cragg, who has influenced not only us but a whole generation in the field. We each mistakenly assumed the other knew the way to the lecture hall. Finally, when we were completely lost, we had to ask a stranger, who showed us the way.

The present volume points out twelve paths to a real relationship between Muslims and Christians. David not only knows them but has walked them all many times. This is the major value of the book. He not only shows the importance of each path but gives examples from his own experience of how he has dealt with the stumbling blocks involved. He clarifies the core similarities and differences between the Christian church and the house of Islam so we know where we converge and where we diverge.

Some paths of relationship are clear—cultivating respect, practicing hospitality, and confronting distortions. Other paths are more challenging—how to live with integrity, have a clear identity, develop trust, and answer questions in contexts where evangelism is forbidden by law and we are guests. The examples he provides and the responses he gave in concrete situations are particularly instructive. Also illuminating is the way he and others he has known have been able to partner with persons of peace—some of whom were originally Muslim militants. Throughout, he merges the paths of pursuing peace and commending Christ.

Years ago in Hartford, when David and I were trying to find where Kenneth Cragg was lecturing, we arrived a little late. Cragg was dealing with how the power of God is best demonstrated. Is it with a clenched fist and the words *Allahu akbar* (God is great) or with the outstretched hand with a nail print in it? For those of us who have arrived a little late, the paths in this volume will lead us to the outstretched hand with a nail print in it.

—J. Dudley Woodberry
Dean Emeritus and Senior Professor of Islamic Studies
School of Intercultural Studies, Fuller Theological Seminary

Preface

Our experiences of greeting and meeting Muslims are exceedingly varied. I have visited many mosques and have had conversations about faith with Muslims within their places of worship. Many readers, however, live in regions where no non-Muslim may enter the mosque. Nevertheless, I hope the basic principles I describe in this book will be helpful to all Christians who are engaged with Muslims, whatever the circumstances might be.

I am a North American who grew up in Tanzania, where my parents were pioneer missionaries serving with a Mennonite mission agency. This heritage influences me significantly. I write quite differently than if I were a Nigerian believer in Jesus the Messiah whose family is Muslim, or a Christian born into the congested urban region of Jakarta in Indonesia. As we consider paths for relationship between Christians and Muslims, I am aware that my experiences are different from those of Christians in the Middle East who represent the ancient Christian churches within predominantly Muslim societies. Every church community has a special gift to offer in the conversation about how to develop real relationship with Muslims. In this book, the twelve paths to relationship are a modest effort to learn and share about the contemporary challenges and realities of cultivating real relationships between Muslims and Christians, with particular reflection on the journey of North American and other Western Christians.

In this book I describe the experience of Western Christians who are committed to being good neighbors among Muslims. In a very real way this book is my story. It is an account of discoveries that I, a North American believer in Jesus the Messiah, have made during many years of relating to Muslims.

I am writing for all who are interested in living and serving among Muslims. I frequently meet Christians who are leaving their homes in the West to live and serve among Muslims. Such people often ask me for advice as they become involved in Muslim communities. I hope this book will be an encouragement as well as helpful counsel for anyone who hopes to cultivate real relationship with Muslims in any region of the world.

I am also writing for Westerners who sense the nudge from God to become engaged with Muslims in their communities. For many Westerners, Muslims have become our neighbors. This book is intended to equip us all, Muslims and Christians, to be good neighbors.

As a resource for those who wish to join in this journey, we have developed three books that compose the Christians Meeting Muslims series. Each of the three books in the series can be summarized in a word or two. *Dialogue* stands at the center of *A Muslim and a Christian in Dialogue*, which I coauthored with Badru D. Kateregga. *Journeys of the Muslim Nation and the Christian Church: Exploring the Mission of Two Communities* looks at *witness* and *invitation*.

And in *Teatime in Mogadishu: My Journey as a Peace Ambassador in the World of Islam*, Ahmed Ali Haile (as told to me) focuses on *peacemaking*.

Each of these books includes study questions. They have thirteen sections or chapters to facilitate small-group discussion or to enhance the value of each book as a classroom text. Each book is a distinctive contribution for those who want to understand the Muslim movement with a Christ-centered commitment.

Why, then, have I put my hand to writing a fourth book for this series? The joys and challenges of Christian-Muslim *friendship* are the organizing focus of this book. I write with urgency, for we live at a time in which commitments to friendship are often severely challenged. This book is complementary to the other three in the series.

I have written this book to stimulate vigorous small-group discussion or to be used as a classroom textbook on Christian-Muslim relationship. The questions at the end of each chapter will facilitate a lively exploration of challenges and opportunities.

I have been enormously enriched in my journey with Muslims. I hope this book will inspire many to likewise enter the joys and challenges of Christians meeting Muslims.

—*David W. Shenk*

Acknowledgments

For some years a small cluster of Anabaptist theologians and missiologists have been informally meeting one day a year in the home of a friend in Elkhart, Indiana, to consider ways we can encourage the church communities we represent, mostly through writing. We meet just before Christmas, and hence we have nicknamed ourselves "The Christmas Theology Circle."

At one of those gatherings our host challenged me by saying, "A book must be written to describe the challenges and opportunities of developing enduring relations with Muslims." Then he encouraged me to write that book, drawing from my half century of engagement with Muslims. That five-minute conversation planted the seeds of this book in my soul.

Many have contributed their counsel. The accounts of both Muslims and Christians working for peace are described. I use no pseudonyms. Nevertheless, most contributors prefer serving in an unobtrusive spirit that is quite unnoticed. For that reason I have been conservative in the use of names.

That conservatism means that I have decided to mention no names in this statement of acknowledgments—with one exception. The steady and enthusiastic support of my wife, Grace, is remarkable. She has not only been a great editor, but she has brought immense reserves of wisdom and commitment into the writing of this book.

Also I mention here one educational institution. Students at the Bethany International University, Singapore, provided valuable critique of the manuscript in a course wherein I used this material as the foundation. The course was on cultivating peaceful relations with Muslims. The insights of these students, mostly from predominantly Muslim countries, were most helpful.

I thank the many friends who invested their time generously in providing counsel as I wrote this narrative of cultivating real relationship between Christians and Muslims. Especially significant have been the participants in Eastern Mennonite Missions' Christian/Muslim Relations Team, Peacemakers Confessing Christ.

Introduction
My Journey with Muslims

My immersion within a Muslim community began in the Mogadishu airport in Somalia. Two days later, my friendship with Muslims began in a high-decibel tea shop in the city center. It was August 1963 when our family disembarked from a propeller-driven DC 3 onto an airstrip along the windy beaches of Africa's northeastern Horn. My wife, Grace, and I had arrived with our two daughters, two-year-old Karen and two-month-old Doris.

Within the hour it took to jostle through the confusing cacophony of immigration, customs, health documents inspection, money declaration forms, shouting porters, and a tremendous discussion on the right tips to pay, we had heard the name *Allah* flung into the air a couple hundred times. We knew we had entered a society permeated with an awareness of the encompassing presence of God.

Our intention was to slip through the Mogadishu airport unobtrusively. We knew Somalia was one of the only countries in the world that was basically 100 percent Muslim. As Christians living in Somalia, we would be a miniscule—albeit noticeable—minority. We had hoped to slip through immigration unnoticed. However, the bantering of the fellows handling our suitcases shattered that notion.

Who are you?
In stumbling English within the bedlam, someone shouted, "Be you Somalia Mennonite Mission?"

"Yes, we are with the Mennonite Mission!" Obviously any notion that we could or should mask our identity was futile.

"Then you be true *wadad* (holy man of God)!" one of the tallest porters surmised, as a dozen people turned to see who this holy man and family might be. Such was our quiet arrival in Somalia. I suppose by evening the whole town of Mogadishu had word that another American had joined the Somalia Mennonite Mission (SMM) team.

That was significant. A year earlier the director of the mission had been killed by a zealous *imam* (religious leader) who was troubled by the presence of the "mission." His personal war began when he heard some young Somalis had declared their loyalty to Jesus the Messiah and had made a commitment to the Christian faith. The manner in which the faith decisions of several students became known caused a stir. Consequently, the mission's educational program had been closed for several months, and new laws approved by parliament mandated that only the true religion of Islam could be propagated in Somalia.

A year later, in 1963, our young family arrived in Somalia to help continue the educational services of the mission. Our arrival was a signal that the mission had no plans to retreat, even in the face of such a tragedy.

Why have you come?

The surprising persistence of the mission raised questions among the Somali people. A common notion was that we must be agents of some colonial power, such as the United States government. That question was the essence of a tea-shop conversation a couple of evenings after our arrival.

Three or four students in our Mogadishu adult English literacy program took me several blocks from our school compound to a boisterous street-side tea shop. Humorously, they confided that evening tea drinking in open-sided kiosks is men's business. Men revel in discussions of grand matters over cups of tea. Nevertheless, some single, female teachers who were serving in our mission accompanied the male students to the tea shop. These women from North America felt one aspect of their presence in Somalia was to push back on some boundaries the male-dominated society had foisted on women.

My hosts ordered spicy tea without milk, sweetened with five heaping spoonfuls of sugar. As we sipped our tea, the students pressed me with a question that was uppermost in their minds. They asked, "Why have you come to Somalia?"

"God called us," I explained simply. "Our family is here by God's appointment. Jesus served those in need. I pray we can also serve those in need. We are grateful you and your countrypersons have welcomed us. It is a privilege to learn to know and appreciate the Somali people."

They were quite surprised that God would have appointed us. They explained that Somalis know about God and that they did not need to be told. If telling people about God was our intention, we should go to the peoples south of Somalia who followed traditional African religions. However, they stressed their appreciation for the medical and educational programs that SMM was developing in several locations.

That was our first half-week's immersion in the world of Islam. I'll come back to our family's story in a moment. For now, let me just say that the immersion and adventures have continued in astonishingly varied ways for some fifty years.

Seeking the rule of God

This book is about adventure, to be sure, but it is more than that. I want to share my heart in regard to Christian engagement with Muslims. This book includes what Muslims have taught me about Christian presence and witness among Muslims. This is not a memoir. Rather, it is a collection of stories about my journey of meeting Muslims and greeting Muslims.

I write this book with the conviction that every Muslim should have a Christian friend and every Christian should have a Muslim friend. Toward that end, this book lays out twelve paths for real relationship between Muslims and Christians. Half the world's population is either Muslim or Christian. These faith families, along with the Jews, believe their faiths originate with God's call to Abraham to bless all nations. This means these faiths carry special responsibilities for peacemaking. The commitment to being a people of peace in our pluralist world is an integrating theme throughout this book.

The question I have discussed with Muslims, beginning with that tea shop in Mogadishu half a century ago, is this: what does it mean for God's kingdom to come on earth? Both faithful Muslims and devout Christians yearn for every area of life to come under the authority of God and his will. Seeking the rule of God is a common strand of faith and intention that might pull us together in some aspects of our work and witness. For example, both communities are mandated in their scriptures to care for orphans.

My church community is Anabaptist. Within the Anabaptist family of Christians, I am a member of the church known as Mennonite, which is a nickname because one of the early leaders was Menno Simons. The worldwide conference of Mennonite churches has identified seven commitments that characterize the Mennonite church.[1] All seven Mennonite commitments have been significant for me as I write this book, but one commitment is especially pertinent to my engagement with Muslims: Anabaptist Christians are committed to bringing all of life under the authority of God.[2]

In the sixteenth century, the Anabaptists' understandings of what it means to bring all of life under the authority of Jesus Christ brought them into serious conflict with the authorities. This is because at that time Europe was at war with the Ottoman Muslim Empire. Michael Sattler, one of the Anabaptist leaders, insisted that Jesus would never kill a Muslim, for Jesus loves Muslims. The Anabaptists generally agreed with Sattler. The refusal of Anabaptists to participate in the wars against the Ottoman Turks was considered treason. Thus, many Anabaptists

---

1. These seven characteristics of Mennonites and other Anabaptists are listed in appendix E. All seven commitments are important, but of special pertinence to this book are the themes of expressing the love of Christ and his kingdom even when that commitment is not popular.

2. Faithful Muslims are also committed to bringing every area of life under the authority of God. Muslims call this commitment *tauhid,* and they believe the Qur'an is the instruction on how to live in *tauhid.* So Muslims and Anabaptists have this in common: the belief that all of life needs to come under the authority of God. The difference is that for Anabaptists, Jesus Christ is the center; for Muslims, it is the Qur'an that reveals the nature of the will of God.

were martyred for their commitment to loving Muslims rather than fighting against Muslims.

What does it mean for me to be a faithful ambassador of Christ and his peace in our tumultuous world?[3] I am writing these lines in June 2014, which has turned into a month of anguish. Boko Haram has kidnapped some three hundred high school girls in Nigeria. The United States is gearing up to provide more military assistance for "moderate" Muslims in Syria. Al Shabab has bombed a market and attacked Christians at worship in Kenya. Christian vigilantes are violently cleansing southern Chad of Muslims. A drone is reported to have killed Muslim militants in southern Yemen. The European Union Parliament is moving toward the right amid concerns about the growing Muslim immigrant community in Europe. There are reports of Boko Haram killing several hundred villagers in Borno State in Nigeria. Shi'ite pilgrims returning home to Iraq have been ambushed and killed by Sunni Muslims in Pakistan. An international air terminal in Karachi, Pakistan, has been attacked by militants. Peace negotiations between the Palestinians and Israelis have fallen apart. Iraq is coming apart in the divide between Shi'ite and Sunni Muslims. In Mombasa, Kenya, a Muslim cleric who was keenly engaged in peace efforts among Somali clans was killed while at prayer in a downtown Mombasa mosque. Pakistan has initiated air strikes against Taliban insurgents. In Egypt, members of the Muslim Brotherhood have been served the death penalty by Egyptian courts.

These thirty days in June are the context in which relationship-building between Muslims and Christians must happen. The astonishment is that the participants in all these conflicts believe they are on God's side. In case we have not noticed, peacemaking is urgent!

Peacemaking and prayer
Is it presumptuous to write about real relationship in times like these? It is not. It is not presumptuous because we know God is committed to peacemaking. God has a plan, and that plan

---

3. Bible: 2 Corinthians 5:18-21.

involves us. As God sent Jesus as his peace emissary, so Jesus is also sending all his disciples to serve as peace emissaries. God's grand plan is to salt the whole world with his peace emissaries.[4]

One example of what I am writing about happened in the midst of the June calamities I have just described. On Pentecost Sunday, June 8, 2014, Pope Francis invited the Palestinian president, Mahmoud Abbas, and the president of Israel, Shimon Peres, to meet with him in the Vatican Gardens for sunset prayers for peace. The prayers focused on three themes common in the prayers of Muslims, Jews, and Christians: thanking God for creation, seeking forgiveness from God, and petitioning God for peace.

The pope's spokesperson commented that within the seemingly insurmountable obstacles for peace in the Middle East, "prayer has the ability to transform hearts and thus to transform history."[5] All three of these leaders profess faith in the God of Abraham, who commissions believers to be a blessing to all nations. They believe peace is the will of God.

Peacemaking is like the little mustard seed to which Jesus refers.[6] Peacemaking begins with tiny steps. For example, recently a coworker organized a weekend boating outing for a couple of dozen Muslims and Christians. They had a hilariously good time! My colleague was planting seeds of peace. It is these kinds of "peace" seeds being planted all around the world that give us hope. This is an example of paths to real relationship.

A bedrock conviction for me is that all these paths for real relations must be grounded in prayer. As I came through immigration in New York just a day ago, the officer said, "With such a fully stamped and used passport, you might as well just buy an airplane and save the money you are paying the airlines for tickets." Paging through the many pages and visas in my passport, he wondered what I do that demands so much travel.

I told him I am an ambassador of Christ and his peace in the church around the world, and I am working especially in

---

4. Bible: John 20:19-22.
5. As quoted by Cardinal Pietro Parolin, Secretary of State for the Vatican. For full article, see Nicole Winfield, "Pope Dives into Mideast Peace with Prayer Summit," *The Big Story*, Associated Press, June 8, 2014, http://bigstory.ap.org/article/pope-kicks-mideast-peace-summit-prayer.
6. Bible: Matthew 13:31-32.

Christian-Muslim relations. Since the church and Muslims are all around the world, I need to travel a lot, I told him. "God bless you!" he exclaimed. "Our world needs more peacemakers, but do not forget the world needs a lot of prayer!"

I believe the officer is right.

The pain and joy of dialogue

Some years ago my congregation in the United States invited me and a Muslim imam to an evening of dialogue. My imam companion drew two partially overlapping circles on the whiteboard. Then in the center of the circle representing the Muslim community, he wrote, "Qur'an." In the circle representing the church he wrote, "Christ." He explained that these different centers mean there can never be complete overlap, for the centers are different.

That is the pain of dialogue. Muslims proclaim the Qur'an is the fullest revelation of the will of God. Christians confess Jesus is the full revelation of God—not just his will, but also the essence of God. Christians confess the Messiah is the breakthrough of the kingdom of God on earth and the one in whom there is eternal salvation. Muslims view Muhammad as the perfect example whom all people should emulate.

So what? Does it really matter whether Jesus or Muhammad is the center?

"It does not matter!" my German seatmate proclaimed with zest on a recent flight from Frankfurt. She resented the Muslim insistence that what Muslims and Christians believe really does matter.

My taxi driver on one of my trips to Singapore would disagree. As soon as we were on our way, he asked, "Do you believe in Jesus Christ? He is the Savior. He is the way!"

Neither would the imam in the mosque in Harrisburg agree with the woman from Germany. At the end of a long evening of conversation, the kindly imam embraced me and wept as he pleaded, "You are too good a man to be a Christian. I implore you to become a Muslim."

In chapter 5 we will explore more carefully these different "truth centers" and what that means in developing respectful relations. In the meantime, I go back to my first evening in a

Mogadishu tea kiosk and to the years that followed. That evening was the first of many such experiences. The conversations in Somalia went on for a decade. Fellowships of believers in the Messiah developed wherever our people served.[7] Recall that in the gospel of John, Nicodemus came to Jesus at night inquiring about the kingdom of God.[8] In our Somali sojourn there were many Nicodemuses. Those were joyous years.

Moving to Kenya

Then, like a rolling thunderstorm slowly gaining momentum across the Somali acacia-studded grasslands, the country we had come to love became a Marxist state with strong Soviet control. On October 21, 1969, lightning struck in the form of a military coup. Somalia became a Marxist-Leninist revolutionary state. The Marxist government quickly extended its tentacles within every aspect of Somali economic and political society. One consequence was that all Westerners had to leave. That was difficult for us to accept, but we trusted that new doors of opportunity for ministry among Muslims would open. Indeed, that happened in Kenya.

So in January 1973, about ten years after our arrival in Mogadishu, we deplaned in Nairobi, Kenya. This country borders Somalia on the southeast. We were now a family of six. We settled into the Somali-Muslim section of the city called Eastleigh. We created a reading room. In the next several years a multifaceted community center and program developed; today the center

---

7. In the Qur'an Jesus is referred to as "the Messiah." This is the Semitic way of saying "Christ." Both the Semitic *Messiah* and Greek *Christ* carry the same meaning—namely, "the Anointed One." Since Muslims are best acquainted with *Messiah*, when referring to Jesus, I will generally use the name *Jesus the Messiah*. However, I recognize that although Muslims refer to Jesus as the Messiah, Muslim theology has not understood the fullness of the meaning of Messiah as revealed in the Bible. I also recognize the Qur'an uses other names for Jesus as well, such as a "Sign," *Ankabut* (The Spider): surah 19:20, "Good News," *Ali-Imran* (The Family of Imran): surah 3:45, the "Word of God," and the "Spirit of God," *Nisaa* (The Women): surah 4:171. Appendix B is a selective list of names for Jesus in the Qur'an. For further discussion of the names of Jesus in Islam, I suggest my book *Journeys of the Muslim Nation and the Christian Church: Exploring the Mission of Two Communities* (Harrisonburg, VA: Herald Press, 2003), chapters 5 and 7. Also, Tarif Khalidi edited and translated *The Muslim Jesus: Sayings and Stories in Islamic Literature* (Cambridge, MA: Harvard University Press, 2001).
8. Bible: John 3:1-2.

touches about one thousand people a week. The services of the center include a significant library; a variety of classes, especially for women; and a sports program with workout facilities. The basketball team is notable; it is called the Menno Knights. The center has developed as a crossroads for peoples across the vast regions of the Horn of Africa. A fellowship of believers has emerged. Several congregations of various traditions meet at the center. Our team wrote a study of the Scriptures that touches hundreds of students every year.

Another surprise of serving in Kenya was the invitation by Kenyatta University College for me to teach the world religions classes in the religious studies department. We trained teachers for the religious studies programs in Kenyan high schools. Significantly, I became a friend and colleague of Professor Badru Kateregga, a Muslim from Uganda who was also teaching in the department. Out of our friendship we authored a book, *A Muslim and a Christian in Dialogue*, wherein he confesses his faith and I respond, and I share my faith and he responds. This simple book of twenty-four chapters has been translated into about a dozen languages, and has been a helpful contribution in cultivating interfaith understanding.

Cultivating relationship with Sufis

The Eastleigh Fellowship Center is across the street from the Sufi mosque.[9] We cultivated relationship with the Sufis, who we believed were a door into the Muslim community, a door revealing spiritual yearnings.

The Sufis are a stream of Muslim spirituality who quest to be absorbed into God. They are generally known as communities of peace. There are four spiritual streams within the Muslim movement that give Sufis hope for absorption into God. First is the belief that one night Muhammad was taken from Mecca via Jerusalem into the presence of God in a mystic journey known as the *Miraj*.[10] Therefore Muhammad is thought to be the

9. David W. Shenk, "The African Christian and Islamic Mysticism: Folk Islam," in *The African Christian and Islam,* ed. John Azumah and Lamin Sanneh (Cumbria, UK: Langham, 2013), 251–72.
10. Qur'an: *Najm* (The Star): surah 53:13-18.

pathfinder, leading devotees into being absorbed into God. The second stream is the assertion in the Qur'an that Abraham was a friend of God (*wali*).[11] The third is the hope that pious saints of the past might be appointed by God to serve as intercessors leading the devotee into absorption within the divine.[12] Fourth is the mystic experience of repeating the name of God over and over.[13] Sufi communities offered the individual a path into absorption into the divine; the communities were also recognized as islands of intercommunal peace within the quite tumultuous Somali clan relationships.

Tragically, the drug culture hijacked the Sufi movement across much of northeastern Africa. That applied also to Eastleigh. In their Thursday night gatherings, chanting the names of God while chewing a euphoria-enhancing plant (khat) was thought to be evidence of authentic absorption into God. These practices spawned apathy and eventually even dementia. Sadly, such unwholesome expressions of spirituality, practiced by so many across northeast Africa, are a smothering blanket on economic and educational development. Of course there were *ulama* (Muslim religious scholars) who pled for expressions of Islam more in harmony with the Qur'an and who decried the use of khat to enhance spirituality.

Our message among Sufis was that the Messiah and the mission of the Holy Spirit fulfill the yearning of Sufis to experience God. But with a difference! The Sufi quest leads to the obliteration of selfhood through being absorbed into the universal. Through the Messiah, the person is not obliterated or absorbed into divinity. Rather the Messiah invites believers into a lively, joyous, and life-giving relationship with God and with one another.

Several times I met with Sufis in their prayer centers and joined in the pilgrimage to the tomb of one of their saints. Meeting with the Sufis opened doors for meaningful conversations, spiritually grounded in Jesus and the Holy Spirit. Muslims viewed the Sufi communities as people of peace.

In partnership with other Christian fellowships, a companion center to the Eastleigh Fellowship Center was developed in

---

11. Qur'an: *Nisaa* (Women): surah 4:125.
12. Qur'an: *Yunus* (Jonah): surah 10:3-5.
13. Qur'an: *Munafiqun* (Hypocrites): surah 63:9.

Muslim northeastern Kenya, in the town of Garissa. That center was modeled on the Sufi approach to community. These two Christian centers, one in Garissa and the other in the Eastleigh, were contextualized expressions of the community of Christian faith within a Sufi environment. Within that context, Muslims appreciated the Christian communities in Garissa and Eastleigh as congregations of piety, prayer, service, and peacemaking.

We cannot overstate the significance of the prayer ministry that emerged out of the center in Garissa. A Canadian sister has been the visionary. A small team joined her in this ministry of prayer for the Somali people. Even in times of conflict and turmoil within the region, they have served in prayer for healing grace. They have persisted, sometimes with lives under threat. There have been martyrs. Miracles have happened; occasionally Jesus would appear to touch a broken refugee woman, revealing himself as her gracious healer. This praying team has patiently persisted in prayer for more than two decades.

A global focus on Christian-Muslim relations

Six years after our arrival in Kenya, it was clear the time had come to leave, in order to give Africans more opportunity to pick up the many responsibilities we carried. We moved to the United States, to our home community in Lancaster County, Pennsylvania. For some years I gave leadership to the Eastern Mennonite Mission (EMM) local and then global missions programs. Within those roles I kept concern for faithful presence and witness among Muslims as a core commitment.

Since I lay aside my administrative responsibilities at EMM in 1998, Grace and I have been engaged in ministry related to Muslims with peacemaking and witness in the way of Christ as our core commitment. A team works with us. We are called the Christian/Muslim Relations Team, Peacemakers Confessing Christ. A first priority for the team is cultivating relations with Muslim leaders in our community. We also write and publish; my books are in over a dozen languages. We work within North America but are also quite engaged internationally; in recent trips to eastern Europe and southeast Asia, members of our team contributed to more than a dozen seminars and dialogues on peacemaking.

About half those events were sponsored by Muslims. A primary commitment of our team is equipping churches to engage Muslim communities in peacebuilding.

Those first conversations in that Mogadishu tea shop and the many that followed were a school of sorts, equipping me for conversations with Muslims that would take me around the world again and again. Most significant, however, was the way that Mogadishu equipped me for the many conversations with Muslims in my American homeland, including neighbors where I live in Lancaster, Pennsylvania.

In this book, as I describe our commitment to cultivating a peacemaking ministry among Muslims, I will regularly refer to episodes in the journey. I hope this account will be an encouragement and will open eyes to new possibilities in the challenging saga of Christian-Muslim relations. I trust the principles of relationship building I describe here will help us relate to Muslims as Jesus modeled in his relationships in the pluralist world where he lived and served.

Questions for discussion
1. Describe your relationship with a person of a different faith from your own. What are some of the surprises of your relationship?
2. Imagine that your job would take you to work in a Muslim country. What do you think some of the special challenges of that venture would be?
3. Faithful Muslims and faithful Christians seek to bring all areas of life under the rule of God. What are some areas in which Muslims and Christians could join hands to work together in that commitment? What are some areas of difference that would make cooperation unlikely?
4. What are the different centers that form the Muslim and Christian communities? What difference do those centers make in the life and mission of the Muslim and Christian communities?

CHAPTER 1

Live with Integrity

The imam in the mosque is preaching against you. Be careful," my friend Farah advised.

We had arrived in Somalia a few months earlier. I responded, "If he has something against me, I must meet him. Give me his name, and I will go to the mosque to meet him now. I have nothing to hide. Please arrange a meeting."

Farah promised to bring the imam to our home. He came with some of his disciples, and Grace served them spiced tea and date cookies. The imam began, "There is a rumor in town that you hope to go to heaven when you die. If that is true, I will tell you how to get to heaven!"

I was astonished! This was not what I expected from an imam who I understood to be preaching against me. With a sense of relief, I responded quite emphatically, "That is absolutely true! Thanks for coming to tell me the way to heaven."

The imam confided, "I thought Christians prefer hell to heaven. But the way to heaven is to submit to the five pillars of duty in Islam: confess the creed that there is no God but Allah and Muhammad is his prophet, fast during the month of Ramadan, give to the poor, pray five times daily, and take the pilgrimage to Mecca, if possible."

"Basically I do these five duties, and I can improve on those where I am weak," I responded. "I would be delighted to go to Mecca as soon as I can make arrangements."

"Praise God!" he said. "You have become a Muslim. Be a secret believer; do not even tell your wife, so that the mission does not stop your salary. And heaven might become your destiny."

I pled, "I need to know my destiny. Please tell me the true way to heaven."

"There is a balance scales," he answered. "These duties go on the good deeds side of the scales. The wrong we do goes on the opposite side of the scales. No one knows which side is the heaviest: the good deeds or the wrong deeds. Even I do not know. However, Islam is the best hope that we know of."

The integrity of the imam impressed me. I was startled by his confession that he had no firm assurance about his eternal destiny. I asked, "May I share with you what Jesus the Messiah says about this? Jesus says, 'I am the way, the truth, and the life.' He promises that he is the way. So which way should I choose? Jesus or another way?"

The imam was amazed. He said, "If Jesus has promised that he is the way, then I urge you to continue being a Christian!"

My friend Farah told me that after that conversation, when the imam heard someone speaking critically of me, the imam would say, "I have drunk tea in the home of David and his wife. We have talked about the deep things of God. And I am confident that man is going to heaven."

That conversation happened in a context where it was illegal to propagate Christianity. Yet the commitment to integrity, which addressed the issues without a spirit of deviousness, opened surprising doors for authentic relationships.

Somalis often describe the Somalia Mennonite Mission (SMM) appointees as people of integrity. The Corinthians apparently said the same of the apostle Paul. He writes that God's people avoid saying no and yes. There is no room for deviance. Rather, Christ is always "yes" to all the promises of God! In the same spirit Paul intended to keep his promises to the Corinthians.[1]

Recall the fellows at the street-side tea shop who probed me with questions as we sipped cardamom-spiced black tea. Hollow answers would not cut it. The Qur'an warns against duplicity. It warns that Christian friendship with Muslims might be a facade with ulterior motives lurking beneath the surface.[2] The questions at the café that evening were not asked in hostility. They

1. Bible: 2 Corinthians 1:17-21.
2. Qur'an: *Mujadila* (The Woman Who Pleads): surah 58:14-19.

were honest questions. The fellows with me wanted to make it quite clear that motives such as bringing about the conversion of Somalis to the Christian faith would not be welcome.

I responded, "I am here by the appointment, or call, of God." That answer intrigues Muslims. A strong theological stream in Muslim belief is that God directs all happenings. Being in Somalia by God's appointment was, therefore, surprising and yet quite comprehensible to them.

Authentic witness

Nevertheless, my tea-table companions were concerned. Could it be that I thought the intention of God's appointment was the conversion of Somalis to the Christian faith? If that was the case, then how could our acquaintance develop into friendship? The whole structure of the *dar al Islam* (region under Muslim rule) is, in essence, to protect the integrity of community.[3] That includes protecting Muslims from any notions of leaving the Muslim community.

Muslims believe they have a duty to proclaim Islam to the whole world. In fact, within the prayer call from minarets around the world, Muslims proclaim their witness and their invitation. Here is an abbreviated expression of the call: God is most great, there is no God but Allah and Muhammad is the prophet of God, so come and experience well-being; come and worship. A Muslim friend told me the prayer call is an urgent witness and invitation to all humankind.

In my walk with Muslims I find it is often quite difficult for them to acknowledge that Christians also believe we are called to bear witness. I have had scores of dialogues with Muslims, often in mosques. The calling of Christians to bear witness, and the freedom for people to accept the Christian invitation, are the

---

3. *Dar al Islam* means "the house of Islam." *Umma* literally means "mother." The Muslim community is known as the *umma*. Four centuries after the formation of the *umma*, the phrase *dar al Islam* came into wide use to communicate the idea of territory and political governance. Although *dar al Islam* began to be widely used in the fourth century after the *hijrah* (the migration of Muhammad and his Meccan followers to Medina in AD 622), the concept of *dar al Islam* is significant within the early beginnings of the Muslim movement. In this text I will use both *dar al Islam* and *umma* to refer to the development of the community; *dar al Islam* indicates an emphasis on the political and territorial dimensions of the movement.

most challenging issues that come my way again and again in dialogue with Muslims.

The community of Islam believes Islam is God's eternal instruction about what we should believe and do. That eternal instruction is unchangeable. This means Islam is the first, middle, and final religion of humankind. How, then, could anyone consider leaving the final religion? It is difficult to find space within the Muslim worldview for anyone who is Muslim to choose another way.

Conversion away from Islam was on the mind of the district commissioner in the town where we moved after our arrival in Somalia. My assignment was to develop a thriving boarding middle school. It was illegal to propagate Christianity. We could not invite students to Bible studies. If someone wanted to engage in a Bible study, we would ask the inquirer to sign a statement saying this study was at their request. Our plan was to show the police these signed statements if we were ever questioned about the Bible studies.

Giving account to the authorities

I was in my midtwenties. I reveled in the challenge and opportunities before us. Then I was brought down to earth by a directive from the district commissioner to appear in his office. The enormous office was filled with people. In the presence of all, the officer confronted me. "It has been reported to me that some of the students in your charge are becoming Christians. That is against the law. I am ordering a full investigation. I can assure you, this will stop!"

I was concerned that an outcry of "*Allahu akbar!*" (God is most great!) might ensue. I prayed silently, "Holy Spirit, Jesus promised you will tell us what to say in such circumstances. So please hurry! There is no time to spare."

I asked to have all those in the office leave, except for one witness. The officer agreed with the good sense of the request. Only the chief of police remained. Then I responded, "I will not comment on whether students have become believers in the Messiah. Only God knows the heart. So do your investigation and decide for yourself what is happening. As for the Mennonite mission teachers, we serve at the school as guests in your country. We are grateful for the privilege of serving and working with the Somali people. As guests we seek to obey the laws of your country.

"However, I have a problem, and I need your advice," I continued. "When I first believed in Jesus the Messiah many years ago, the Spirit of God filled me with joy and love. I cannot ignore this gift from God. Occasionally a student comes to me saying, 'I see in you the gift of joy and love. I believe the gift comes from the Christian faith within you. Please explain this faith to me and lead me to become a believer.'

"What should I do? If students come to me asking for a Bible study, what is the right response? If you wanted to believe, could I or the government prevent you? Are you not after all a free man? How should I respond to these students?"

The commissioner interjected, "You are right. I am a free man. No one can determine my faith for me. As for the students, continue just as you are doing. You are doing well. There will be no further investigation."

That event was a trust-building asset. The trust was developed upon the foundation of truthfulness. On one occasion I was with a high-level government education officer—I believe he was the minister of education. At that time I was the director of the mission. I told him we were committed to openness and integrity in all areas.

Then I commented, "We as the Somalia Mennonite Mission want to serve in ways that are respectful of the laws of the land. That is a special challenge for us in the light of the law prohibiting propagating the Christian faith. So I would like to share how we seek to work within the law."

He replied, "No, do not tell me how you function. We know how you function. Continue as you are doing. If you make a mistake we will inform you. But do not make mistakes."

Go home if you hope my people will become Christians

A key aspect of integrity in Muslim societies is addressing the prevailing suspicion that evangelism is the real motive for the arrival and presence of Christian service personnel. Recall that this was the first question that came my way at the street-side tea kiosk in our early days in Somalia. It was also the concern of the officer who was launching an investigation into our school with regard to students becoming Christians. The suspicion often lurks that the reason for the Christian presence is evangelism, not just service. This was the concern we met in Somalia.

Christian witness was also the concern I encountered in the Philippines. Colleagues and I were visiting in Mindanao in the southern Philippines, where there have been episodic wars between central government forces and Muslim separatist groups. One of the Mennonite agencies had placed a Canadian peace emissary in that village. We were introduced to the village and then had a fine dinner in the home of the sultan as a tribute for the work of the peace emissary.

During the dinner several of the sultan's sons broached the question with nervous coughs. "What is the real reason for your presence in our town?"

Their kindly father, the sultan, pressed the matter further. "I am the descendant of many generations of sultans, whose responsibility generation by generation has been to assure that this town remains Muslim and no one leaves the Muslim community to become a Christian. We appreciate the work of your emissary, but if perchance you are hoping persons from this town become Christians, that is religious imperialism, which I will never tolerate. In that case you should go home!"

Of course, for the sultan, Christianity meant much more than belief in Jesus. He viewed Christianity in the same way he viewed Islam, namely as a comprehensive geopolitical system. In Mindanao those different systems had been in conflict for decades. For him anyone who was joining Christianity was joining the imperial system of the enemy. It is for that reason that, in conversation with Muslims, I usually avoid identifying myself as a Christian. Rather, I refer to myself as a believer in Jesus the Messiah.

We were rather shaken by the broadside from this gentle and pious sultan. It was obvious that he feared our service might be a tool for proselytizing. Some of my Christian colleagues might respond to such concerns by declaring, "Oh my, no! We would never expect a Muslim from your village would become

a Christian. We are only here as service workers. We would discourage any Muslim from becoming a Christian."

What, then, happens if a Muslim does decide to become a
Christian? Huge questions of trust burst into the arena. The integrity of the service workers would indeed be in question.

Since I was the fellow with the gray beard, eyes turned to me
to respond to the sultan. I silently interceded, "Lord, lead out in
this conversation!"

I began, "Thanks for expressing your concern. I want to make
four comments. First, we all agree Christians and Muslims should
never proselytize. By that we mean using money or other induce-
ments for people to change their religion. We abhor and condemn
such practices anywhere in the world.

"We agree with the assertion in the Qur'an: 'Let there be no
compulsion in religion!'[4] The Bible also proclaims the freedom
of the person to choose without compulsion: 'Let the one who
wishes take the free gift of the water of life.'[5]

"Second, Muslims frequently invite me to become a Muslim.
They do this because they appreciate me, and they believe Islam
would be a great blessing for me. Christians likewise yearn that
others also come to believe the gospel.

"Third, we all realize none of us can convert anyone; conversion is between a person and God.

"Fourth, we are here as guests by your invitation, and when
you feel we should leave, we will leave in peace.

"Our emissary has come as a servant of Jesus the Messiah
who has taught us to love, even our enemies. In fact, Jesus even
washed the feet of Judas who was a traitor. We believe the love of
the Messiah brings healing to a person and to a community. We
are here to bear witness to the healing love of Christ.

"Suppose someone in your town would decide he wants to
join us in commitment to Jesus the Messiah and wants to walk
with us in loving service even for his enemies. What if we would
refuse the person and say that only we who are guests among
you can believe in and follow Jesus, and no one else is permitted to join with us in the journey? Would that not be religious

---

4. Qur'an: *Baqara* (The Heifer): surah 2:256.
5. Bible: Revelation 22:17.

imperialism to say, 'Jesus the Messiah is only for us, and not for others'?"

The response was immediate and emotional. "Oh, no! You cannot say only you may believe in Jesus the Messiah. That would indeed be religious imperialism. You are right. Jesus is for everyone!"

Ask the Christian

Several years later, the young men in the sultan's village were preparing for battle with the governing authorities. They were storing arms, but before launching the attack, the leaders met with the sultan for his counsel and blessing. The sultan told the warriors to go and ask their Christian guest for his advice.

The guest from abroad was surprised when the warriors preparing for battle came asking his counsel. He advised the warriors to go and pray and hear what God was saying about the proposed war. They came back later and said they had heard nothing from God. So he advised them to leave and pray some more. After some days of this back-and-forth-for-prayer scenario, they told the Christian, "God has spoken and said we should not go to war." So the warriors sold their weapons and put the cash into developing a school!

The transformation in attitudes was astonishing. The sultan, who earlier said our emissary should go home if we hoped some in the village would become Christians, was now advising the young men to seek counsel from the Christian on whether to go to war or desist. I suppose this is what Jesus meant when he said his disciples are the salt of the earth. Although a church had not yet emerged, the salt of the kingdom was transforming the community through the Christ-centered presence and witness of an emissary of the Messiah.

The salt of integrity

To be a person of integrity is to sail against the wind in most societies. We experience counterwinds in subtle as well as bold ways. For example, at the school in Somalia students frequently performed hilarious dramas. In one of these dramas an illiterate nomad comes to town for a day and leaves his money in the mosque with the *wadad* (an illiterate folk religious leader). In the evening the nomad comes to reclaim his money, but the *wadad* feigns insanity and cannot understand what the nomad wants. So the illiterate nomad returns home bereft of his money. The drama was hilarious. The next day in classes, students debriefed the drama. The overwhelming notion was that the *wadad* did the right thing, for he had outwitted the nomad. I was dismayed. I had hoped that our presence as Sermon on the Mount believers was necessary "salt" and "light" that would encourage an integrity that was not assumed by the society as a whole.

However, the Muslim faculty and theologians on the staff were as appalled as we were with the response of the students. Integrity was a virtue they also sought to inculcate in their teaching of Islam. Those theologians who knew Islam were aware of the dire warning within Islamic teaching: if anyone accuses another falsely, the accuser shall be punished with the same punishment the falsely accused would have suffered. Opposition to false witness flowed deeply within the Muslim societies with whom we worked.

So, within our schools Muslim and Christian spirituality joined hands to instill in the students an integrity critiquing the values of the *wadad* in the play. The Christian presence seemed to call forth renewed commitments by the Muslims among whom we served to cultivate an appreciation for integrity. This is why Muslim Somalis often commented, "We trust you!"

Jesus referred to his disciples as "salt" and "light."[6] Christian presence everywhere, including in Muslim societies, must be grounded in integrity. The salt of integrity is what I observed in a visit to central Asia where a Christian acquaintance was developing a chicken business. With a team of fellow believers, he established a feed provision outlet for the developing chicken-raising businesses in the region. Farmers raised the grain and then brought it to the outlet for mixing and processing for feed. The community named the scales weighing the feed "the truth scales." That feed-selling business earned the reputation throughout the entire region as an honest business.

---

6. Bible: Matthew 5:13-16.

The salt and light of integrity need to permeate all areas of life. For example, some countries will provide visas for businesspersons or those in professions such as teaching English. The visas are provided for a particular business or profession, but sometimes the appointee never actually begins a business. She might have a business facade, such as a name card and registration certificate, but no business. Or an English teacher might be teaching only several hours a week, but not enough to justify a visa. When visas are granted for a particular vocation, it is imperative that the recipient invest generously in the vocation for which the visa is provided. When authorities learn of the dubious use of visas and expel workers, we should not accuse the authorities of being anti-Christian when in fact they are simply requiring the service worker to function with integrity.

When a person is entering a country for the purpose of mission, I believe it is wise to register as a mission if possible. That was our stance in Somalia. And that was not only our stance. Other church-related agencies also generally registered as "mission," or some designation of "Christian service." We were the Somalia Mennonite Mission. In due course forty people were issued visas for service in a country that was realistically 100 percent Muslim. Each visa was linked to a service the government approved. I served as the director of the SMM schools. My wife acquired her visa as a homemaker. All of us in the education department of the mission were committed to serving with excellence. Our schools acquired the reputation of being the best schools in the country. We developed a first-rate high school, in addition to elementary and middle schools, and a strong adult education program. We were known as the education mission.

We viewed commitment to excellence as a sign of the kingdom of God. Our schools were like a show-and-tell, and the whole nation was impressed with our commitment to excellence. Our schools were not a facade. They were not a camouflage for evangelism. We answered questions about faith. Fellowships of believers emerged. That was not a secret. But the emerging church was unobtrusive. Our presence was a total lifestyle of commitment to integrity.

We were not the only Christian organization serving in Somalia. Excellence was the hallmark of each of the several Christian agencies who contributed to the development of the country. In fact, I believe that around the world Christian service agencies are generally recognized and appreciated for excellence and compassion.

Innocent as doves

Of course, we use discretion in explaining who we are. Sometimes I wear the hat of a pastor. In Somalia I was usually a teacher. Other times I am a university professor or a scholar. Or I might be a tourist; in that case I do some authentic tourism. Some will go as businesspersons and do business. We seek to be prudent in all involvement. It is rarely wise to "wave flags." Unobtrusive service in the name of Christ is wise, but we avoid deviousness. That commitment takes us into the next chapter: keep your identity clear.

Jesus counseled, "Be as shrewd as snakes and as innocent as doves!"[7] As always, advice from Jesus is good advice.

Questions for discussion

1. Compare the restrictions Christian teachers experience in Canadian or U.S. public school systems with restrictions to Christian witness in many Muslim societies. How best should Christian teachers function within such restrictive systems?

2. Freedom of religion is a key issue in Christian engagement with Muslims. What approaches do you suggest in confronting this critical issue?

3. How do you respond to the assumption in this chapter that service and bearing witness belong together? How do you respond to the commitments to integral service and witness presented in this chapter?

---

7. Bible: Matthew 10:16.

CHAPTER 2
Keep Identity Clear

During the United States' occupation of Iraq, I participated in a gathering of eighty Muslim and Christian leaders in Central Java, in Indonesia. I spoke on the peace of the Messiah. Then a question came from the back of the room.

"You have described the Messiah as the one who forgives his enemies and thereby breaks the cycle of revenge," the person said. "But your president, George Bush, claims to be a Christian, and he has led your country into a couple wars. We are confused."

The political order and the kingdom of God

How would you respond?

The Indonesia moderator of the meeting rebuked the questioner, saying, "It is quite impolite to challenge a guest in this way!" But I assured the moderator that I did not take offense, for this is an important question, and one deserving a clear response. This is what I said:

"I am here as an ambassador of Jesus the Messiah, not as a representative of the United States government. I am here by God's grace seeking to represent the kingdom of Jesus the Messiah, which is eternal and is grounded upon the suffering, reconciling, forgiving love revealed in Jesus, who on the cross cried out in forgiveness for the sins of the world.

"Nations come and go. Empires rise and fall, and nations and empires go to war. These wars are a revelation of our sinfulness. However, the kingdom of God is eternal and it is a kingdom grounded in the life-giving love of God. Before the war in Iraq began, the community of churches of which I am a member sent a letter to President Bush imploring him not to go to war. The letter had seven thousand signatures. We tried to deflect the United States government from going to war, but we were not heard. May God forgive us for not doing more!"

I learned later this speech was broadcast on national television. This was an important statement, for Christian witness must be clear that the kingdom of God is not the political order of nation-states. Disciples of Jesus have their identity in Jesus the Messiah and his kingdom. The church is a sign of that kingdom.

We admit this is a challenge, for we are also citizens of nations. How do we live faithfully to the Messiah and his kingdom while also being citizens of nations? I admit this reality presents special challenges to Christians. Yet our ultimate loyalty needs to be to the kingdom of God, not to the kingdoms of this world.

The challenge of maintaining a clear identity is with us when serving anywhere in the world. In this chapter we look especially at the identity questions that come our way as we live and serve in Muslim societies. The conversation in Indonesia described above is one example of the challenge.

How we handle identity is very much related to integrity. Identity and integrity are different sides of the same coin. Identity has been a concern in Christian-Muslim relations for some 1,400 years, ever since the Muslim movement began.

Running through the soul of the Muslim community is the sense of Muslim "otherness." There is the world of the Muslim *umma* on the one hand, and the world that is not *umma* on the other hand. This reality of otherness is evident when the Muslim congregation gathers for the five-times-daily prayers. Muslims explain it to me this way: "Each line of worshipers standing foot to foot is a wall, shutting out the world of non-Islam while facing the *Ka'bah* [a small, cube-shaped building in Mecca containing a sacred black stone]. We do this simultaneously with all other Muslims around the world." The symbolism of the prayer time communicates that there are essentially two communities: the community of Islam and the community of non-Islam. The side-by-side, foot-to-foot line of worshipers is a wall protecting the *umma* from outside threats.

Christians also believe they are called to reject the sinfulness of the world. Jesus said his disciples are in but not of the world.[1] The church symbolizes its otherness from the world in the weekly gathering for worship. The otherness of the church from the larger society is expressed in many ways, but especially in baptism and confirmation. Those events communicate that the church is a distinctive community in a world of many communities.

This otherness stream in both the Muslim and Christian movements means that cultivating trusting relations is a special challenge. For this reason, Christians who want to be accepted by the Muslim community are often inclined to mask their Christian identity, especially when they are a minority in a Muslim society or nation.

Encouraging one another

Obviously, Muslims living in pluralist Western societies also experience enormous pressures to conform. Parents worry that their youth will succumb to the allures of Western culture. A provocative insight into these pressures is the book *How Does It Feel to Be a Problem? Being Young and Arab in America.* The author, Moustafa Bayoumi, describes the lives of seven young Arabs living in Brooklyn. Yasmin is one of them. She was a committed Muslim, born in Brooklyn. In her junior year in high school, this *hijab*-wearing teenager ran for student council president. She won the election. She reveled in her responsibilities. Then came the first school dance. Yasmin respectfully informed the administration that, in good conscience, she could not attend.

The administration demanded that she resign; their policy was that the council president had to attend the dances. She looked for support in every direction, including the New York City Board of Education. She hit a brick wall at every turn. She was completely alone in her battle. The book mentions no Christian student stepping forward to encourage her in her lonely struggle. She had no alternative except to resign. Then an immigrant lawyer entered the fray, with a simple letter reminding the administration that the U.S. Constitution guarantees freedom of conscience. The administration took the challenge seriously and suspended the

---

1. Bible: John 15:18-19.

regulation on student council presidents attending dances. The next year Yasmin ran again and won the election a second time. She was then reinstated as student council president.[2]

This young Arab Muslim gently and boldly stood firm in her identity amid enormous opposition and disappointment. I wonder where the Christian students were! Lending moral support to Yasmin could have been an immense step in encouraging a young Muslim who was eagerly committed to standing on her principles while also earnestly serving the country her family had adopted.

Like Yasmin, Muslim women who have scattered around the world in recent years often dress with distinctive Muslim garb. So do many Muslim men. A *kufi*-wearing imam told me that traveling overland from Canada to the United States can be an adventure. Crossing borders where his *kufi* (skullcap) distinguishes him is a sign of pride in his Muslim identity. These Muslims want to boldly reveal they are distinctive.

Avoid camouflage

In contrast, identity camouflage is what I observed several years ago when I was in central Asia enjoying a chat with a young Christian service worker from the United States. He was quite excited about sharing an incident that week.

He told me, "The young men I hang out with asked me a very interesting question. They asked me why I do not womanize and drink."

"What a great question!" I exclaimed. "What did you say?"

"I told them it is because women and alcohol are not to my taste!"

I could not mask my surprise. "It seems to me this was a wide-open door for you to share the gospel and your choice to follow Christ in a commitment to chastity and righteous living," I probed. "Why did you not enter this open door by bearing witness to the new life in Christ?"

"Oh, I could not do that," he exclaimed in surprise at my comments. "That would have blown my cover. I am here on a business visa. I cannot let the secret out that I am a Christian."

---

2. Mustafa Bayoumi, *How Does It Feel to Be a Problem? Being Young and Arab in America* (New York: Penguin, 2008), 83–114.

I queried, "What are you here for? Suppose an angel were to appear to someone in this town and give an instruction, which occasionally does happen in Muslim societies. Imagine this command: 'Go and find a Christian and ask him to tell you about the Messiah.' Would that person know that you are a Christian and he should come to you in obedience to the instruction of the angel?"

This dear young man who had left family and home to serve Christ in central Asia told me that as far as he knew, no one in the town was aware he was a Christian.

In dramatic contrast to the young man's camouflage, an Asian businessman told me he places his identity in Christ in writing on his office wall. He lives in a restrictive situation. He has followed through in registering his company fully in accord with the laws. On the registration certificate, one must state the name of the CEO. He has placed Jesus Christ as the CEO of his company. Regulations state that the certificate must be displayed on the office wall.

Many customers and fellow businesspersons ask him, "Who is this Jesus who is the CEO of your company?" He has many opportunities to share the gospel, and in fact has led people to faith in Christ right inside his office. His company is prospering. He has acquired considerable wealth that he invests in Christian ministries.

Identity in the church of Philadelphia

Of course, most of us do not post a sign declaring we are Christian. But we need to be transparent about our commitment to Christ and his church. Revelation 3:7-13 contains a remarkable statement about identity in the message of the angel to the church in Philadelphia. The angel promises that for this church, Jesus will open a door no one can close. For our purposes I consider this as a promise for an open door for engagement with Muslims. (Chapter 12 contains a more extensive discussion of the open doors for the church in Philadelphia.)

Not all the churches described in Revelation are given the gift of an open door. In fact, it is only the church of Philadelphia for whom the door is opened. Why? It is significant that this church has a clear identity. There are several statements, all of which are about identity:

1. The participants of this church are pillars. They stand firm.
2. The name of God is upon them. They are known as the people of God.
3. The name of the city of God, the New Jerusalem, is upon them. This city is the church. People know the participants are identified as members of the church.[3]
4. Jesus himself also seals their identity by placing his name upon them. This is what happened in the early church. People nicknamed the believers "Christian." They were recognized as Christlike people.

The church has its foibles. No church is perfect; all churches have their cracks. I often hear Christian service workers make comments that they would not want to introduce Muslim-background believers to the local church because of the church's shortcomings. It is true that the local church sometimes falls short; I know that our international Christian-Muslim relations team certainly does.

However, the church is the only community in the world that confesses the grace of God in Christ, and therefore it is a community touched by joy. This is the reason Christians always sing when they meet together for worship. Of course, in some places underground churches need to mute their singing. The local church is the only community in town that meets in the name of Jesus and celebrates his life-giving presence.

Jesus has promised, "For where two or three gather in my name, there am I with them."[4] Amid its cracks and failures, Jesus stands in the midst of the church, touching the worshipers with his renewing grace.

---

3. *New Jerusalem* has several meanings. One meaning is the church. The name probably also relates to the kingdom of God, which has a broader meaning than the church. The meaning of the New Jerusalem merits more comment than is possible in this short book, so hereafter I will refer to the New Jerusalem and the city of God as the church.
4. Bible: Matthew 18:20.

Clarity of identity can open doors

In my global travels I am often asked what my vocation is. I usually respond this way: "I am a Christian who seeks to serve Christ in his mission of healing and hope for the nations." Frequently I include my denominational affiliation. This is because church identity for me is universal but also specific.

Some years ago I was invited by an association of Muslim students in the United Kingdom to participate in public dialogues, mostly in universities. When I arrived at Heathrow Airport, I asked my host why they were inviting me.

He said, "Because of who you are."

"Who am I?" I prodded.

He replied, "You are committed to Jesus Christ. We see that in your books. We appreciate Christians who know where they stand and are clear about their commitment to Christ."

Identity when visiting a mosque

It is not always possible to visit mosques. In some countries or locations doing so is not advisable. But in the United States and in East Africa, where I lived for some years, it is possible to visit mosques. I always ask if I and a group of Christians may come and enjoy conversation after the prayers. I never join in the *salat* (ritual prayers). I think that would hopelessly confuse my identity, for they would all think we are Muslims. Rather, we sit in the back, observing the prayers, and praying quietly for the Holy Spirit to take part in the conversations. After the Muslims have concluded their prayers, we sit in a circle and the conversations begin. Occasionally the conversation moves toward Jesus the Messiah. It is as though Jesus invited himself into the circle and in many ways is actually presiding. I suppose I have visited a couple hundred mosques over the years. I do not recall any visit where Jesus was totally ignored. Time after time I leave those engagements thanking God for an open door to bear witness for Jesus. And I have always been invited to come back again!

I do not think that would be true if our identity were not clear. I think my host for the rambunctious dialogues in the United Kingdom got it right. I am welcome because I believe in Jesus the Messiah.

Objections to masquerading

Some of my Christian colleagues believe obscuring our identity
will open more doors. I do not judge those who go in that way.
However, I bring two concerns to the table. First is the Qur'an
itself, which is critical of those who masquerade as Muslims but
are in reality Christians. I believe we need to take this objection
seriously. We can understand the objections. What if a Muslim
were to come to my church masquerading as a Christian, and in
due course we entrusted him with a Sunday school class, only to
find he is teaching the children that Muhammad is the Seal of the
Prophets? We would be quite disturbed.

The second concern is what happens in our own souls when we
embrace a fuzzy identity. My friend Ahmed Haile used to say putting one foot in the church and the other in the mosque is to have
a divided mind. Some well-meaning church leaders in Muslim
communities will place the Qur'an and the Bible side by side in
the front of the place of meeting. What does that communicate
about identity? Is it not saying that the Bible and the Qur'an have
equal authority? Is that not building a divided house? Can such
a house endure?

The mosque is not the church. The Qur'an is the center of the
mosque. Christ is the center of the church. When Muslims and
Christians meet in dialogue with one another, they are speaking
from a commitment to the authority of the Qur'an, on the one
hand, and the authority of Christ on the other. A healthy dialogue
respects the reality of those different centers. In the next chapter
I will comment on contextualization of the message. Here I just
note: healthy contextualization does not wash out differences,
but rather acknowledges the different centers.

Some disciples of Jesus refer to themselves as "Muslims" or
as "Muslim believers in Jesus." Of course, all Muslims believe
in Jesus as a remarkable prophet. I suppose Muslims have told
me in a thousand different settings, "You believe in Jesus and
Muslims believe in Jesus, so we are all Muslims."

So to say, "I am a Muslim believer in Jesus" just confirms
the Muslim assertion that all of us, at the end of the day, are
Muslims. Technically, that is true, for the name *Muslim* means
one who believes in and submits to the peace of God. But what is

the peace of God? Is submission to the Qur'an the same as believing in Jesus Christ? I do not believe that is true. So for me to say I am a Muslim believer in Jesus enormously confuses the biblical witness that Jesus the Messiah is Savior and Lord. The biblical confession that Jesus the Messiah is Lord and Savior is not what Muslims mean when they proclaim belief in Jesus.

Identity and place

One cannot divorce identity from place. For Islam, that place is the *Ka'bah*. For the church, the place is wherever the people of God meet in worship; there is no *Ka'bah* in the Christian movement. What, then, shall we say about the place known as the church building? In Indonesia the church reaching out in mission to Muslims generally takes two different approaches to the identity that place gives.

Some argue an established building is necessary when reaching Muslims. They believe the building is a statement that the community of faith is not a transient phenomenon but rather an established movement; the church building is a sign of permanence. The largest Mennonite church building in the world is in Semarang, Java, and accommodates twenty thousand people. It is often filled to capacity; people mostly from a Muslim background are coming to faith through the witness of this outreaching church.

Others who live within another context in this same nation have a different take on the issue of identity and a church building. For them it would be impossible to develop a church building within an energetic Muslim environment. So these believers worship unobtrusively in homes. Their music is locally developed. The small, unobtrusive nature of these fellowships helps to provide space for the church within a tight Muslim community.

But in both settings there is a clear commitment to identity. Both meet in the name of Christ and confess he is Savior and Lord. The mosque recognizes that these Christian communities are not Muslim. They are Christ-centered fellowships or congregations.

Symbols communicate identity

The symbols and practices of a church within a Muslim context should bear witness that the Messiah is the Savior who has come from heaven. The symbols and practices of the mosque proclaim that the Qur'an is a gift from heaven. In their sincere commitment to commend the Messiah in acceptable ways for Muslims, some Christians use Islamic rituals, such as bowing toward Mecca in prayer. They might encourage converts to the Messiah to remain in the mosque. When this is the practice, what is being communicated within the Muslim environment? Are these symbols and practices perceived to be saying there really is no difference between the mosque and the church, between the gospel and Islam? When we try to emulate Muslim symbols and practices, does that not sow seeds of confusion?

People become believers in Jesus because they have found new life and freedom in Jesus. Islam does not offer the grace and joy of eternal salvation. People do not come to Jesus because he offers much the same thing Islam offers. Let us remember that our identity is in Christ! No symbols can adequately communicate that reality; "in Christ, life" is the gift of the Holy Spirit. Christians break bread and share in drinking wine or juice as symbols of faith centered in Jesus, crucified and risen. Islam invites faith and commitment to the revelation of God's will that first came down in the environs of Mecca; that is why Muslims face the *Ka'bah* in prayer.

Discerning identity in Mogadishu

A remarkable series of conversations about the role of place and worship practices took place in Mogadishu some years ago. Twenty Somali believers in the Messiah gathered every Friday morning for about a year for conversations about practices in the church. They wanted the church to be contextual to the Muslim-Somali cultural and religious environment. International participants were welcome.

Every situation is different. The Mogadishu experience had particular realities that would not apply elsewhere. Nevertheless, I share the broad outlines of the decisions made by this group of Somali believers. This account is significant, for it describes the manner in which a particular congregation worked through contextualization questions. I believe the way they worked at the questions is more significant than the decisions they made. In the New Testament, we read that the church convened a similar kind of meeting in Jerusalem to look at questions related to Jewish and Gentile practices.[5] That meeting is called the Jerusalem Conference. The believers in Somalia had a similar meeting: it could be called the Mogadishu Conference!

The group decided to call themselves the Somali Believers Fellowship. Some used the term *people of the Messiah*. They avoided using *Christian*, for that term had so much Western baggage. They also avoided using denominational names.

They decided to take the cross out of their meeting place because it appeared to be a potentially idolatrous symbol. They also decided they would not bow in prayer, for bowing in Islam is always toward a place—namely, the *Ka'bah*. In contrast, Christians worship God as our loving heavenly Father. In that culture, sons stand to communicate with their fathers. So as sons and daughters of God, they decided the most appropriate posture for prayers in the church should be standing. They decided to regularly pray the Lord's Prayer as a chant, which would be a replacement of the *Fatiha* they had prayed as Muslims.

Recognizing that in their Muslim context the confession of faith is significant, these believers decided to adopt the Apostles' Creed as their confession. They liked that creed, for it represented the universality of the church as well as the historical foundations of the church. Acknowledging that Somalis are noted for their pride and intransigence, they decided there would be occasional footwashing rituals in their church, emulating Jesus, who had washed the feet of his disciples. They felt this was important as a practice, radically cutting across their cultural motif of never touching another's foot! For communion they elected to use sweetened colored water when possible; otherwise they were quite ready to use camel's milk.

The Somali believers were committed to making sure that the symbols of their worship and life would show identification with the worldwide church. So they decided to worship on Sunday, as

5. Bible: Acts 15:1-35.

a symbol of participation with the universal church that generally meets for worship on Sunday. Later the authorities forbade meeting on Sunday, and so they met on Friday.

The Somali believers were small, scattered fellowships. Most of the international participants serving in Somalia were with the Mennonite church. Although they did not call themselves Mennonites, the Somali believers fellowships cultivated relationships with the global Mennonite church. That relationship assured them that they were participants in a worldwide family of believers. They needed those connections. Visitors coming from abroad, and leaders of the fellowship visiting churches abroad, were an important encouragement.

They gave high priority to developing indigenous songs that had lyrics with traditional alliteration. They tried to acquire a building as a place to meet and connect, but it was soon evident that this would be impossible because of community opposition. For a few years the believers met in the Somalia Mennonite Mission center. When the SMM properties were taken by the Marxist revolutionary authorities, a Catholic cathedral provided a special meeting room just for the Somali believers.

They were also concerned about leadership. They encouraged the person leading the weekly worship to stand as he led, and to wear dignified attire. In due course one from among the believers was ordained as their pastor. He was able to represent the body of believers well to the governing authorities; he was also an effective preacher and teacher of the Word.

Debates about contextualization

The discussion forty years ago about being both Somali and believers in the Messiah is related to discussions about *contextualization*. Issues surrounding contextualization are debated intensely today among missiologists serving within Muslim societies. Mission leaders often think of contextualization as a continuum they refer to as the C1–C6 spectrum. A Muslim believer on the C6 end of the scale is a person who professes faith in the Messiah while remaining fully rooted in the mosque and Muslim practices. On the other hand, C1 believers have left their Muslim heritage and have become fully integrated into the life of the international church. The discussions in Mogadishu never mentioned the C1–C6 spectrum; such concerns were not much in vogue forty years ago.

In reality, however, the decisions we made in Mogadishu would fit quite well within a C4 framework. We were becoming the Somali Believers Fellowship, with roots in Somali culture but clearly identified as being the people of the Messiah.

A key question in the C1–C6 debate is whether a believer in Jesus the Messiah should continue worshiping in the mosque or whether she should leave the mosque. The discussions in Mogadishu I have described led to a consensus. The fellowship encouraged believers in Jesus to leave the mosque. However, they developed rituals and worship patterns that communicated the gospel within their Muslim context.

For example, bowing toward Mecca as the worshiper recites the *Fatiha* is central to Muslim worship. In contrast, when the believers' fellowship met, they stood for prayer as sons and daughters stand before their fathers. The recitation of the Lord's Prayer replaced the *Fatiha*. The Apostles' Creed became their confession of faith. These are examples of contextualization wherein believers seek to develop within their Muslim environment meaningful forms of worship with a Christ-centered focus.

Muslim-background believers are not of one mind about this. In Mogadishu a key leader probably expressed the mind of the congregation well when he said, "The mosque is not the church, and the church is not the mosque. The day I believed in Jesus the Messiah is the day I stopped going to the mosque for prayer. To continue in the mosque is to live with a divided mind."

Another believer in Sudan told me, "As a believer in Jesus I continue worshiping in the mosque, but instead of repeating the Muslim creed as I worship, I confess in my soul that Jesus is Lord and Savior. By staying in the mosque I find many doors open to share the gospel that would never open if I left the mosque."

There you have it! The great debate goes on.

Let us not enter the debate uninformed, however. I have been very much formed by the experience and theology of Ahmed Haile, and I commend his book, *Teatime in Mogadishu*.[6]

---

6. Ahmed Ali Haile, as told to David W. Shenk, *Teatime in Mogadishu: My Journey as a Peace Ambassador in the World of Islam* (Harrisonburg, VA: Herald Press, 2011).

The gospel of freedom

The Mogadishu fellowship repeatedly returned to the account of Jesus meeting the woman of Samaria at the well. Jesus and the Samaritan had a lively dialogue about true worship. In the midst of conversation, Jesus declared, "God is spirit, and his worshipers must worship in the Spirit and in truth."[7]

For the believers in Mogadishu, this statement by Jesus was enormously freeing and life-giving. They rejoiced that the gospel freed them from the requirements of Islam. It also freed them to develop their own forms of worship within their context. At the heart of it all was knowing God in spirit and in truth as their loving heavenly Father.

Questions for discussion

1. In apostolic times Christians often worshiped in Jewish synagogues or in the temple. What are the positives and negatives of Muslim-background believers worshiping in the mosque?
2. Consider the decisions of the church in Mogadishu as it discerned relevant contextualization in its setting.
3. What are some ways a Christian international service worker can help facilitate the need of a young Muslim-background congregation to connect with the worldwide church? Why would that be important for an emerging church within a Muslim society?
4. What are some of the reasons identity is important? Can you think of situations where it might be wise and right to hide one's Christian identity?

---

7. Bible: John 4:24.

CHAPTER 3

Cultivate Respect

Some four hundred Muslims jammed the central London mosque for a dialogue I had with a well-known Muslim cleric. It was a three-hour marathon that engaged key theological challenges. This was the church and the house of Islam encountering one another. Especially sharp was the confrontation with Islamic Christology, which is quite divergent with biblical Christology. In the conversation, the Muslim cleric ruthlessly critiqued the core of the gospel—the life and teachings of Jesus, the incarnation of God in the Messiah, the crucifixion of Jesus, and the resurrection. I prayerfully sought to confess Jesus the Messiah in his fullness as clearly, as winsomely, as persuasively, and as forthrightly as possible.

The next day my Muslim dialogue companion surprised me. "Last evening you confessed the gospel with forthright clarity, even though in doing so you were challenging core beliefs of the Muslims in the mosque," he observed. "Everyone sat with focused attention. No one left. There were no shouts of 'Allahu akbar!' The entire congregation listened. Do you know why?"

"Please tell me," I invited.

He observed, "We listened because you love and respect us. If you would not respect us, we would have shouted you down. You not only respected us, but you also avoided any attacks on the Qur'an or Muhammad. If you would have used the podium to attack Islam, we would never have listened to you."

Recall when I had arrived in London for this series of dialogues, my host had said they invited me because I was committed to Christ. He had also made another comment. He said, "We rec-ognize you love and respect Muslims." Indeed, a respectful spirit opens doors for relationship building as well as bearing witness to Christ.

For most in the mosque that evening, this was the first time they had heard the gospel. I believe they were astonished by this amazing good news. Had I been disrespectful, the door for wit-ness would have closed.

Cherishing mutual respect

Of course, respect should be a two-way street. During my eve-ning in the London mosque, I expressed my dismay about what I felt was disrespect for the Bible from my Muslim companion. I observed forthrightly, "I have not come here to attack Islam, the Qur'an, or Muhammad. I am here to present the gospel. And I request that you reciprocate the respect I am expressing by not attacking the Bible or the beliefs of the church. We can disagree. In fact, if we are faithful to our different spiritual foundations, we *will* disagree. But I implore you, even in disagreement, be respect-ful of biblical faith. The Qur'an nicknames us 'The People of the Book,' meaning the Bible. We like the nickname, for we believe the name was given to us by the early Muslims because of our respect for the Bible. In fact, the Qur'an warns us to not depart from the Scriptures God has entrusted to us."[1]

Respect does not require that we agree. In fact, I am grieved by some of the misrepresentations of Jesus I have sometimes ex-perienced in my walk with Muslims. This leads me into soul-searching; do I misrepresent Muslims? Generally the Qur'an has high respect for Christians.[2] The respect that Muslims have for Christians is often related to the respect that Christians have for Muslims.

Yet there are ample warnings as well. There is judgment in the Qur'an against those who spurn Islam after they have heard the truth of Islam. The Qur'an is also quite ruthless in its con-demnation of hypocrites who publicly confess their loyalty to the Qur'an and Muhammad but in reality reject Islam.[3] Such people

---

1. Qur'an: *Maida* (The Table Spread): surah 5:65-66.
2. Qur'an: *Maida* (The Table Spread): surah 5:82.
3. Qur'an: *Maida* (The Table Spread): surah 5:51, 54, 57.

do not have a sincere heart. Muslims are told they need to be cautious about Christians who seek to be friends of Muslims but do not believe the Muslim scriptures.

What do you think about Muhammad?

On a visit to southern Asia, a local pastor and his associates took me to the *madrassa* (Muslim place of learning), where the imam and his colleagues were teaching Islam to about fifty students. We had a most congenial conversation. We were in the building, and the students congregated outside. Their faces crowded in the two windows of the room where we were meeting. They listened with reverent and curious attention. I am sure this was the first time Christians had appeared at the *madrassa*. The pastor had lived in the community for a couple of decades and had never visited with the Muslim leadership in the town. The Christian leaders were afraid they might offend the Muslims, so the Christian and Muslim leaders just avoided each other.

The conversation was cordial as both leadership groups sought to get acquainted. Then the imam turned to me and asked, "What do you think of Muhammad and the Qur'an?" How should I have answered? Actually, I appreciated the question, for it opened the door to confess the salvation we have in Jesus, a gift Muhammad and Islam do not offer.

I responded, "Thank you for a very important question. I have high respect for much that Muhammad did. For example, he confronted injustice such as the practice in his society of abandoning female babies. He also confronted idolatry. By the time of his death, most of the Arabian people had abandoned the worship of polytheistic gods. During his lifetime the Arabian people turned from polytheism to worship only God almighty, the creator of the universe. All of this is remarkable.

"I also want to say a word about the biblical witness concerning Jesus the Messiah, for I stand upon the Bible. Beginning with Adam and the prophets, whose teachings are preserved in the Bible, we read that God would someday send a prophet who would be the Truth and the Savior from sin. The prophets promised all who believe in him would receive the forgiveness of sin and the gracious gift of eternal salvation. Many years ago

I believed in Jesus the Messiah, and indeed through him and by God's grace, I have received the gift of salvation. With deep gratitude I confess that my sins are forgiven and my destiny is eternal life in the presence of God.

"So the question in my soul is whether Muhammad and the Qur'an bear witness that Jesus the Messiah is the one who is the Truth center, the Savior of the world. Or does Muhammad take us in a different direction? As for me, my prophet and Savior is Jesus the Messiah. He is the center of my life, in whom I have received the gift of eternal salvation."

They thanked us cordially and invited all to return for further conversations before long. The question raised in the *madrassa* is a good question that tests our commitment to respectfulness while also providing an open door to share the mission of Jesus. Some Christians will urge forthright discussion about some of the qualities of Muhammad that concern us because they are not in harmony with the character of Jesus. However, a critique of the character of Muhammad is not helpful and in fact will close doors.

I prefer a Messiah-centered response, encouraging people to consider whether Islam is consistent with the biblical witness in regard to the Messiah or whether Islam takes us in a different direction. I like to respond in ways that open the door for the congregation to ponder the question, who is Jesus?

Avoid building walls

An acquaintance conducts seminars on Muhammad in Muslim regions of Africa. He is critical of both the Qur'an and Muhammad. In the African communities where he speaks, a backlash can bring about disaster. Likewise, some negative comments about Muhammad by prominent American church leaders have on occasion been carried in newspapers in the Muslim world. The consequence, in some circumstances, has been great dismay and anger on the part of Muslims.

On one occasion I was in a restaurant in Asia. A pastor in a far corner recognized me and walked over to my table. He said, "I have a message for Christians in America. Just shut up. You make these pronouncements about Muhammad, and the wrath of the local Muslim community falls upon us. We implore you to stop this irresponsibility."

We should use our speech in ways that build respect and trust. This does not mean to ignore concerns. But our expression of concerns must be expressed in ways that build up peaceful relations and do not tear down. I will resist repeating some of the unkind comments about Muhammad and Muslims that circulate widely in Western media. The tragedy is that too often derogatory comments come from the mouths of church leaders. The Bible commands us, "Whoever would love life and see good days must keep their tongue from evil and their lips from deceitful speech. They must turn from evil and do good; they must seek peace and pursue it."[4]

The Qur'an and the Bible

Happily, there is much in the Qur'an and Muslim traditions that is favorable to Christians and to other communities of faith as well. The Qur'an observes that God has created a world of pluralist cultures and religions so that Muslims will learn to be respectful in a pluralist world.[5] This is an explicit command to Muslims to cherish the opportunities for respectful relations in a multicultural and multireligious world.

I want to linger for some time on the respect the Qur'an has for the Bible. (See appendix C for a quite comprehensive listing of statements in the Qur'an in regard to the Bible.) In the Qur'an, Christians are referred to as the People of the Book who are to be respected. Jews and Christians are considered to be those in possession of the former scriptures. The Torah, Psalms, and Gospels are specifically mentioned in the Qur'an as revealed scriptures. Muhammad is commanded to ask these people in possession of the former scriptures any questions he might have.[6] Christians are commanded not to hide their Scriptures but to make them freely available. Christians should stand upon their Scriptures, for if they do not, they will have nothing to stand upon. I recognize there are those Muslims who vigorously insist that the

---

4. Bible: 1 Peter 3:10-11.
5. Qur'an: *Maida* (The Table Spread): surah 5:48; *Hud* (The Prophet Hud): surah 11:118.
6. Qur'an: *Yunus* (Jonah): surah 10:94.

Bible is not trustworthy. But those objections are not found in the Qur'an, wherein the Bible is respected as Scripture that has been entrusted to Christians and Jews.

However, we discover caveats. There are verses in the Qur'an that warn Christians not to obscure their Scriptures. There are charges that some people actually write and peddle false scriptures. Another verse worries that Christians might hide their Scriptures. It is significant that the Qur'an commands Christians to stand upon their Scriptures and to make these writings freely available. Furthermore, although the Qur'an does not charge Christians with changing the written text, it does warn all people not to tamper with scripture.

Nevertheless, although the Qur'an respects the Bible, there is a widespread assumption among Muslims worldwide that the Bible has been altered from its original state. In contrast, they believe that the Arabic Qur'an is an exact replica of the heavenly original. That reality creates special challenges in Christian-Muslim dialogue.

Many Muslims memorize the entire Qur'an. Through the centuries the finest artists in the Muslim world have put their hands to intricate calligraphies of the Qur'an. This book forms civilizations. Imagine the shock, dismay, and anger when Christians disparage the Qur'an. I am not suggesting Christians should accept the Qur'an as revealed scripture. The divergences between the essence of the Qur'an and the essence of the gospel show that one cannot accept both books as equally authoritative scripture; the messages are different. Christians stand upon the Bible, not upon the Qur'an.

But that does not mean we approach the Qur'an disrespectfully. I am impressed, for example, that in the Qur'an Jesus is called the Messiah and he is born of the virgin. So I will respectfully listen to the Muslim understanding of what the virgin birth of the Messiah means in the Qur'an, and then invite them to hear the witness of the gospel in regard to the meaning of the virgin birth and the messiahship of Jesus.

Our family was host to an Iranian Shi'ite family quite recently. With anticipation they joined us for Sunday morning worship. However, the husband of the home felt compelled to stand at the back of the church rather than take a seat on a bench in the auditorium. The reason was that he discovered that Bibles were tucked into a little shelf under the seat. He could not bring himself to sit on the Bible. After church, he sought opportunities to counsel church members to desist from this cavalier attitude toward the Bible.

For Muslims, the Qur'an must be the highest object in the room; if there is a Bible in the room it also must be placed at a place indicating high respect. For this reason I avoid taking my Arabic-English Qur'an with me in a briefcase when I am planning to meet with Muslims. I will take my English version of the Qur'an; in English it is not considered to be an authentic Qur'an. For Muslims, it is only the true Qur'an in Arabic. In handling the Bible and the Qur'an, I resist ever putting the Bible or the Qur'an on the floor. Surely a gift of the Muslim community to the church is a call to handle our Scriptures and those of other traditions with utmost respect.

Objections to a spirit of respect

Some Christians will object to this call for a respectful approach toward the Qur'an and Muhammad. A colleague once told me if there is a little poison in a jar of water, the whole jar is poison. He argues that if the Qur'an does not accept the incarnation, crucifixion, and resurrection of Jesus, then how can I say there are signs of the gospel in the Qur'an?

For example, the Qur'an asserts the virgin birth of Jesus. I believe the virgin birth is true and that it is a sign of the gospel. My colleague disagrees with this approach. The approach I commend is similar to some of the early church fathers in their attitude toward Greek philosophy. It is true that some church fathers such as Tertullian believed there was nothing of worth in Greek philosophy. Other fathers, however, such as Clement of Alexandria, believed philosophy was a preparation for the gospel. He acknowledged that within philosophy there were some themes contrary to the gospel. Nevertheless, he saw the hand of God in the philosophical critique of polytheism.

I commend Clement's approach. In all our efforts to bear witness to the good news, we should "stand on our tiptoes," peering into the Muslim movement in expectation of seeing ways in which the Holy Spirit has planted seeds of truth. These seeds of truth are preparations for the gospel.

Discerning signs of the gospel

We seek these signs in the Qur'an in full recognition of the human inclination to distort and turn away from the gospel. As I read the Qur'an, I grieve over the ways it has not comprehended, or even denies, the gospel. The Qur'an has missed the saving grace of Jesus. Then we meet those passages in the Qur'an that have a violent edge, especially with regard to those who are the aggressors against Muslims. Peace-loving Muslims and Christians grieve the ways militants use these Qur'anic injunctions to justify their violent ways.

At the same time my heart is filled with praises to God for the many ways the Qur'an includes preparatory signs of the gospel. I pray my eyes will be open to ways God has been preparing Muslims for the gospel. In missiology we call such signs *redemptive analogies*. If we disrespect the Qur'an, I fear we shall miss noticing those signs. The signs are not the gospel, but they are an invitation to Muslims to come and explore this man who is the mystery figure of the Qur'an. According to the Qur'an, Jesus is a sign to all nations. Who is this man? We invite our Muslim friends to receive the gospel witness that will clarify the meaning of these astonishing signs about Jesus in the Qur'an.

People of the Book

A disrespectful spirit toward Muhammad and the Qur'an will only build walls of suspicion and hostility between Muslims and Christians. Disrespect will also close the eyes of Christians to ways the Holy Spirit has prepared Muslims to hear the gospel, sometimes through the pages of their own scriptures.

An acquaintance of mine has occasionally gone into Taliban areas of Afghanistan and Pakistan to talk about peacemaking. His credentials: he is known as belonging to the People of the Book. The Taliban recognized their scriptures' command to be respectful of these "People of the Book."

I have found that saying to Muslims, "I am a person of the Book" opens doors. Building upon Qur'anic calls for respect for the People of the Book is a wise approach we should practice in all our relations, and especially so in regions of conflict. If the Qur'an calls for respect for the People of the Book, how much more so should emissaries of the Prince of Peace, whose name is Jesus the Messiah, commit to cultivating peaceful relations?

Christians and Muslims would do well in their relations with one another to emphasize the spirit of goodwill toward Christians that is generally evident in the Qur'an. Goodwill began early on in the Muslim era, when Muhammad sent three hundred of his followers to Ethiopia to be protected by the Christian king Armah Negash. Although Negash never became a Muslim, his open arms to receive and protect the Muslims are a testimony, down through the centuries, which Muslims and Christians should respectfully emulate.[7]

Questions for discussion

1. Consider approaches to Muslims that contribute to building walls.
2. What are some of the open doors for creating respect that are found within the Qur'an?
3. How do you answer these questions: What do you think of the Qur'an? What do you think of Muhammad?
4. How should Christians use the Qur'an in Christian-Muslim dialogue? What are some unwise ways to use the Qur'an? Give examples of using the Qur'an in a wise manner.

---

7. Alfred Guillaume, *The Life of Muhammad: A Translation of Ibn Ishaq's Sirat Rasul Allah* (Oxford: Oxford University Press, 1998), 146–55.

CHAPTER 4

Develop Trust

We trust you!"
During our years in Somalia we heard that exclamation frequently. In a society where interclan and interpersonal trust was often painfully shattered, the statement that the Somalia Mennonite Mission (SMM), a Christian North American philanthropic enterprise, was trustworthy was a treasured affirmation.

Foundations for trust

Why were we trusted? Perhaps it was the many hours of drinking tea and chatting together. We became close friends to many. Perhaps it was our candor and integrity. Perhaps it was our love for the Somali people. Perhaps it was the way we entered Somalia and the way we served. When the mission first entered Somalia, the emissaries exploring possibilities met with government leaders and asked them whether there were needs in Somalia that a church mission organization could help meet. The resounding answer was education. In a society of 90 percent illiteracy, basic education was a crying need. In due course our mission was serving in six locations. In each setting, it was local leaders—the people at the village level—who defined what we should and should not do. We did not set our agenda; the locals did.

Recall that in 1973, when we left Somalia, our family settled into the congested Eastleigh region of Nairobi, which was predominantly Muslim and Somali. We did simple grassroots inquiries as to needs in the community. Consistently, from one end of Eastleigh to the other, the request was for a reading room and library. Homes were mostly one-room affairs; students had no-where to study. We responded to that invitation, and soon as many as eighty students crowded the rooftop reading room. That simple gesture—responding to a need for space to study in the evenings—transformed the academic success rate of students from that whole area of the city.[1] We developed trust through a spirit of hearing what the local people hoped for and then finding ways to work together to bring the hope to pass.

Intentional steps toward building trust

Several years ago a Christian international development agency serving in a thoroughly Muslim context invited Badru Kateregga and me to facilitate conversations about the faith basis for community development within the Christian and Muslim movements. They told us that all their international staff are Christian and all the local staff are Muslim. They were mutually apprehensive of discussions about faith, yet they all knew that faith was foundational to all they were doing in development work. However, they could not talk about faith unless they trusted one another. Our assignment was to help that happen.

We spent two days with about thirty Christian and Muslim staff members. The focus was on faith foundations for peacemaking. Our textbook was *A Muslim and a Christian in Dialogue*, which we had written together. We began our two days together by having the Muslims and Christians meet in separate groups. Each group discussed what they appreciated about the other group and then reported back what they had shared. The Muslims were astonished by how much the Christians appreciated them. Likewise, the Christians listened with amazement to the many ways the Muslims appreciated them.

Most listed friendship high in their considerations, and all spoke of the commitment to God characterized by their companions. That event set the tone for our days together. Each group functioned in the security of knowing they were appreciated, so they felt free to discuss areas of faith and companionship they had never dared to share.

---

1. See the introduction for more about the development of the Eastleigh Fellowship Center.

The most painful dimensions of our two days together occurred when Badru and I each shared the pain we experience in
our relationship to each other, a pain grounded in our different
faith commitments. Badru shared that he grieved because I do not
believe the Qur'an is God's final word of revelation. I shared my
grief in that I have never sensed that Badru considered the possibility that Jesus is the Savior whom God has sent.

This gathering concluded with some forty imams from across
Somaliland meeting with us for a feast. Badru and I were each invited to make statements. He spoke on the need for understanding through dialogue. I spoke about ways Mennonite Christians
and Muslims have worked together for the uplift of children, a
commitment that Jesus models and that the orphan Muhammad
was deeply concerned about.

At the conclusion of the evening, the two leading clerics for
the whole region presented a proposal to me that they would
each marry one of my granddaughters, thereby binding in a covenant the wonderful relations Muslims and Mennonites have enjoyed among the Somali people over the last sixty years. This
was a solemn proposal that, from their perspective, would be an
enormous step forward in Muslim-Christian relations.

I thanked them for their proposed step toward building trust.
I assured them that a matter of such importance needed to be
affirmed by my granddaughters' parents. Of course, we grand-
parents—and our granddaughters—might have some thoughts
on the matter as well!

A revolutionary presence

The trust we enjoyed was remarkable, especially because our
presence was quite revolutionary. This was especially so in regard
to the women in the SMM team. Recall that a couple of SMM
women joined in drinking tea in the street-side tea shop just after our arrival. Their presence alone was quite revolutionary.
Their work was astonishing in a society that believed the place of
women was in the home. The women serving in the SMM team
were professionals who taught business, directed educational
programs, and managed medical ministries. Their work was challenging and highly noticed.

I overheard a conversation between a woman on our team and a young businessman. "We believe our women should work in the home," he said. "That is their place."

The woman responded, "The home is good. But God also opens doors for women to do work that they enjoy outside the home, like becoming a medical expert like me!"

Somalis observing the women on our team would sometimes remind me of a Somali proverb that says, "A mother rocking her baby leads the whole nation!" The men knew that the women in our team, through their example, were pioneering a women's revolution that would permanently transform Somali society. The trust the women on our team earned was vital if the transformations they modeled were to be received with appreciation.

The mothers on our team were vital trust builders, for their vocation was similar to the expectations for a mother in a traditional Somali home. As was true in all the SMM families, Grace, my wife, often went into town with our children to visit in Somali homes. Those relationships developed into a sewing group for Somali women. Weekly, a group of women or teenage girls would come to our home for their sewing circle. And they chatted! The memory of that sewing group is one of Grace's fondest recollections of our years in Somalia. The joviality of those times together genuinely built trust and created friendships.

To Somalis, singleness was a surprise, as were the blessings of monogamy and joyful family life. The director of our bookstore discovered that the most popular book on her shelves was *The Christian View of Family*. When students saw the fiftieth anniversary picture of Grace's parents and their ten children on the wall of our living room, they often asked, "How many women has your father had?"

Grace would reply, "My father has never had any woman other than my mother."

Students would exclaim, "We have never heard of such a possibility: one man and one woman for fifty years. That is so good!"

Who pays you?

Often I was asked, "Where do you get the funds to operate the SMM and the varied development programs?" A general assumption of those who did not know us was that our funds came from some branch of the United States government. We did get funds from Germany and the Netherlands to build the high school in Somalia, but not from the United States. Rather, our funds were derived as our people met together for worship, usually on Sunday mornings, in a couple of hundred churches, mostly in eastern Pennsylvania. These funds were given voluntarily in thanksgiving for God's grace, with a desire to share the love of God around the world by serving people in need.

Many serve internationally in business or the professions. For some years my salary came from a Kenyan university in Nairobi. Others served as researchers and businesspersons. There are countless ways for Christians to become engaged in Muslim communities with support systems that are authentic. The key commitment is to be engaged in ways that the Muslim community affirms and welcomes.

Of course, agencies have varied ways of contributing, and different sources of income. Some agencies do receive government funds. However, my strong preference is a clear church connection with funding. I find it helpful to be able to say, "We acquire funds from Christian friends or from churches." Whatever the sources of income might be, and whatever the nature of the service of international personnel, transparency builds trust.

Islam in the curriculum!

In Somalia one of the most definitive developments in trust building occurred when the government required that Islam be taught in our schools. This was an enormously challenging development. Our partner evangelical mission decided to close their schools rather than submit to this requirement. For the SMM, a critical question was the counsel of the small fellowship of believers in Somalia. We believed that the local church, no matter how small and fragile, must carry a primary role in coming to a decision.

By this time, in the early 1960s, there were several clusters of believers. The believers counseled us to accept the requirement of the government, stating that the gospel is the power of God, so we have no need to fear Islam. They observed that even though Islam would be taught in the classrooms and there was prohibition against propagating Christianity, the Holy Spirit was not bound.

For our supporting constituency in the United States, which was conservative, this was a surprising development. Many were dismayed; their gifts for mission in Somalia would be used to operate schools where Islam was taught. The bishops called for a day of fasting, and then our mission agency's leaders and bishops met for prayer and discernment. Key to the discussion was the counsel of the emerging church in Somalia. When they heard the believers' recommendation, the overwhelming decision was to accept the government policy and to cooperate fully by receiving government-appointed teachers of Islam into our schools.

That decision was a watershed. The whole nation perceived we were in Somalia to serve the people and not to fight Islam. The fellowships of believers continued to develop in remarkable ways. The trust-building act of permitting Islam to be taught actually seemed to provide *more* space for the church to develop and thrive. Somali believers occasionally told me that the trust and appreciation of the government for the mission provided an umbrella under which the church could serve the Somali people fruitfully.

At the school that I directed, as the number of believers increased, we needed more space for gathering than our living room provided. With the believers, we renovated the auto garage into a little chapel room. Then the Muslim students requested a place for them to perform their prayers as well. At that time the high school was being built with German funds, so some of those funds were used for a little prayer house for the Muslims. Thus, it came to be that our school had both a small mosque and a chapel. This was also a trust-building development. We had not anticipated these directions would emerge. But following the Holy Spirit and hearing the counsel of the emerging church took us in directions we would never have imagined. Trust building was writ large over all these developments.

Money for favors?

Our first chapter was on integrity. Trust building requires integrity. We never bribed. We never gave under-the-table money to a government official. We never accepted funds to pry open a door for a student who was not qualified to enter our schools. Our staunch position in such matters did not always earn friends, but it did earn us a trust-building reputation. I acquired the nickname "Tree." The students and parents complained that I was unmovable, like a tree. But I knew that if we budged on protocols, the trust level in the school would plummet. We would become just another school catering to friends and influence and money.

Bible studies and imams

Trust building was also significant in the delicate challenges of conversion and bearing witness to the gospel. For example, in Nairobi a team of seven worked with me for four years in developing a Bible study tailored to the Muslim worldview. When the curriculum was completed we took it into Muslim areas of Kenya and invited Muslim students to take the course and evaluate it.

We referred to the Qur'an occasionally in the course. We were concerned lest our use of the Qur'an be a distortion of the Muslim scriptures or offensive to Muslims. Yet we also thought that principled references to the Qur'an could build trust. We observed there were signs of truth within the Qur'an. As already mentioned, a noteworthy and helpful sign is the Qur'an referring to Jesus as the Messiah; yet we also realize the Qur'anic understanding of Jesus as Messiah diverges from the biblical witness.

We are dismayed when Muslims preach Islam from the Bible. We believe that is a distortion of the biblical message. Likewise, Muslims are dismayed when Christians manipulate the message of the Qur'an. So in our use of the Qur'an, we were determined to not distort its message. This does not mean we did not refer to the Qur'an, but our invitation to Muslims was to hear the biblical message.

One key person we asked to evaluate the course materials was a Pakistani cleric. He would preach near our center in Eastleigh, attacking the Christian faith we proclaimed. Several times we had him and his disciples in our center for dinner and conversation about the gospel. He was an energetic debater. So I took the course to him.

"I do not want to do anything in the Muslim community you do not know about, for I want to have a trusting relationship with you and the Muslims among whom we live," I explained. "This is a Bible study written for Muslims. We have quoted the Qur'an occasionally. Please evaluate the course. Look at our use of the Qur'an to see if we have distorted the message of the Qur'an or if we have been disrespectful of Islam. We are not asking your authorization to distribute the course, because freedom of religion is assured in Kenya. But we do not want to function in ways that are offensive to the Muslim community. I will return in two weeks for your critique."

After a cup of tea, I left him. Two weeks later I returned.

The cleric thanked me for giving him the opportunity to critique the curriculum and then commented, "This is a remarkable course describing the Christian faith very accurately. I would never want to discourage Muslims from understanding what Christians believe, so I will support the circulation of this course in our community. In fact, I must say your use of the Qur'an and comments about Islam are excellent. You have said nothing offensive or untrue about Islam. However, the third chapter of course one made me exceedingly chagrined. It disturbed me greatly." He proceeded to tell me in detail about how that chapter was wrong.

I was taken aback by the vehemence of his objections, which related to the chapter about the human condition. In Islam, Adam made a mistake that can be corrected through instruction. Adam does not need a Savior, for he is fundamentally good. In biblical faith, Adam and Eve and all humanity have turned away from God. We need more than instruction. We need a Savior; we need salvation.

I asked the imam to help me rewrite the segment he objected to so strongly. Together we worked through the thorny patch. We stated that in their disobedience to God Adam and Eve were choosing to turn away from God. All of us participate with Adam and Eve in turning away from God. As we turn away from God we experience separation from God, sinfulness, and death.

At the end of our work together, my turbaned Muslim consultant said, "I disagree with the theology, but I can understand what you are saying." It was remarkable: this cleric, who preached Islam on our street with his loudspeaker, was now helping me to explain the gospel in ways Muslims would understand.

The decision to have Muslims critique the *People of God* course enhanced the acceptability of this Bible study. We also invited extensive Christian counsel. One consultant was a Christian with a PhD in Islam. This was a four-year project, but our Christian scholar engaged with us month by month. Several on the writing team were Muslim-background believers. The entire team was committed to better communicating the gospel. The course has now been touching East African Muslims for several decades, with thousands of courses circulating throughout East Africa. In fact, it has been translated into some forty-five languages. As far as I know, there has been only one objection to the course as it circulates among Muslims.

In an Asian country, shortly after the Bible study was released, the national newspaper ran a front-page feature article about the course, suggesting that people might think it is Muslim material when really it is Christian. The article explained how people can know it is Christian material by describing the message of the course. In this way, people had the opportunity to read about salvation by reading the newspaper description of the curriculum!

A key reason for the acceptance of this course is that we do use the Qur'an when we are confident we are not making the Qur'an say something that is not intended. So the way we use the Qur'an builds trust. We do not attack the Qur'an, nor do we suggest that the Qur'an is communicating the fullness of the gospel. Rather, we view the Qur'an as Muslim scriptures in which there are signs of the gospel.

Halima vouches for the gospel

Relationships are more significant, however, than getting every theological nuance just right. People would enroll in the course and then write to say that they would not know if the curriculum was any good until they met one of the writers or people involved. That is where Halima became especially helpful. Halima was an Eastleigh Somali, a petite and gracious sixteen-year-old. She enjoyed being with our family and then asked Grace to teach her the Bible. Grace and Halima met regularly, exploring the gospel with the *People of God* on the table. Before long, during one of these sessions, she exclaimed, "I am a believer in Jesus!"

About that time, a brother living five hundred miles away came to Eastleigh. He heard of her faith decision and beat Halima severely. She met with us for prayer, asking God especially to help her fully forgive her brother.

She wanted to serve her Savior by sharing the good news across Kenya. With her steady and winsome spirit, hundreds of courses were distributed. Those who came to the office met Halima; her radiance and joy assured all who met her that this was indeed a good course.

Sharing the gospel within a Muslim worldview

As we developed the Bible study, we imagined climbing a ladder. The beginning of the course is the first rung in the ladder. Each lesson is another rung in the ladder, taking us closer to the top, where the student comes to an understanding of the gospel, or hopefully a commitment to Christ. If a rung is spaced too far from the previous rung, the student will fall off the ladder. So in each lesson we imagine our student friend climbing the ladder step by step. We try to keep each rung reasonably spaced above the previous rung. We write in a way that the student views each rung in the ladder as an adventure rather than as a threat. The written responses to the course by those who have completed this study show that, for many, this course has indeed been a surprising adventure into the good news through the biblical narratives.

A significant bridge from Islam to the gospel is the scriptures we use for the course. The scriptures, beyond the Qur'an, that Muslims are most acquainted with are the Torah, the Psalms, and the Gospels. So we mostly use those scriptures. We open the series with the assertion, "God revealed the Torah." The first book in this four-book series is based on that scripture.[2] There is much curiosity about the Torah among Muslims. For example, the Torah tells the Abraham account in a much fuller way than the Qur'an. The nature of biblical narrative amazes many Muslims.

---

2. Qur'an: *Ali Imran* (The Family of Imran): surah 3:3.

We use the Qur'an discreetly. For example, as we have already mentioned, the Qur'an states Jesus is the Messiah. But the Qur'an does not communicate the full meaning of Jesus as Messiah. In fact, the Qur'an asserts the Messiah had a limited mission, for a limited time, and only to Israel! So we simply note that the Qur'an asserts Jesus is the Messiah. Then we invite our Muslim reader to see what the Scriptures God has entrusted to Christians reveal about Jesus as the Messiah.

There is nothing disparaging of Islam in this approach. In fact, the Qur'an says the Messiah fulfills the former scriptures. So inviting a Muslim to explore what the Bible says about Jesus is in harmony with the assertion in the Qur'an that Jesus fulfills the scriptures.

From trust to belief

Several years ago when visiting Singapore, I mentioned this course in a seminar I was teaching. A man stood at the back and waved his hands for attention.

He exclaimed, "I am here because of that course! I am from Lahore in Pakistan. Someone gave me this Bible study course. I met Jesus as I studied these Scriptures and the helpful commentary included in the course."

How did it happen? The approach to the Qur'an and the Bible that our team developed built trust. From the trust came interest and a readiness to hear and receive the gospel message. Critical to the whole journey of the man from Lahore was the trustworthy person who introduced him to the Bible.

The apostle Paul writes, "How, then, can they call on the one they have not believed in? And how can they believe in the one of whom they have not heard? And how can they hear without someone preaching to them? And how can anyone preach unless they are sent? As it is written: 'How beautiful are the feet of those who bring good news!'"[3]

---

3. Bible: Romans 10:14-15.

Questions for discussion

1. What are some of the obstacles to developing trusting relations between Muslims and Christians?
2. Consider specific steps that can be taken to cultivate trusting relationships.
3. Two Christian agencies operated schools in Somalia when the edict came to have Islam taught in their schools. One agency closed its schools; another accepted the edict of the authorities. Discuss the pros and cons of these two different responses. What would you decide if placed in a similar situation?
4. What is your response to asking a Muslim cleric to comment on a Bible study course? What are the strengths and cautions about referring to the Qur'an in a Bible study course?
5. Discuss the ladder approach when introducing the gospel among Muslims.
6. Think of ways that you and your church community can develop trusting relations with Muslims.

CHAPTER 5

Dialogue about the Different Centers

What is the church? What is the house of Islam? We need to pause to clarify those two questions. This chapter is about the church meeting the house of Islam. What are the implications of the different centers that form the house of Islam and form the church? We are aware that there are significant similarities between the two communities.

When I go to a mosque or a synagogue, I feel differently about the experience from when I enter a Hindu temple with its myriad gods. This is because the Hindu temple has not experienced the Abrahamic imprint.

The Abrahamic faiths

The Abrahamic faiths believe in one God who is the creator of the universe and who is personal, righteous, transcendent, and almighty. That is an enormous shift away from worldviews that perceive the universe to be one with divinity. Remarkably, the Abrahamic faiths comprise half the world's population. And the adherents of these faiths believe they have a mission in the world. In the Torah we read that the mission of the Abrahamic family is to bless all nations. Muslims express this calling differently; Abraham is to be an imam over the nations. Yet blessing is implicit or explicit for all these faiths that claim Abraham to be their faith father.

So before further descriptions of discoveries in my walk with Muslims, I will examine the nature of the two houses that compose the Muslim community and the church. What is the nature of the house of Islam? What is the nature of the church? We need to revisit and explore carefully the centers that form these faith communities.

The house of Islam: the *umma*

Umma means "mother." The Muslim community is called *umma*. The community is the caring mother of Muslim believers. The house of Islam is the construction of the community. I will use both *umma* and *house of Islam* in referring to the Muslim community.

The house of Islam comprises twelve pillars (some Muslims would say ten pillars). There are six pillars of belief and six of duty, making a total of twelve pillars upholding the community of Islam. Wherever you might meet Muslims around the world you could ask them, "What are the beliefs and duties of Muslims?" If the Muslims know the faith of Islam, they will respond, "There are five pillars of belief [perhaps six] and there are five pillars of duty [perhaps six]." Below I summarize each pillar.

The six pillars of belief

1. *Belief in one God.* Muslims speak of the ninety-nine names for God, the one and only God. Each *surah* (chapter) in the Qur'an except the first one begins, "In the name of God, the most gracious and the most merciful." These qualities of compassion are most significant in the Muslim understanding of God.
2. *Belief in the prophets.* All the biblical prophets are included, as well as thousands of other prophets. Every people group on earth has prophets. Muslims believe that Muhammad is the seal of the prophets; he is the final prophet who clarifies all other prophets, but his finality is inclusive of all 124,000 prophets who have served people around the world.
3. *Belief in the books of God.* Several books are explicitly mentioned: the Torah, the Psalms, the Gospels, and the

Qur'an. Islam also includes the Scrolls of Abraham as scriptures that Abraham received and wrote down. However, Muslims believe the scriptures Abraham received have been lost. Muslims believe that Christians and Jews possess former scriptures, but Muslims recognize the Qur'an as the final book of revelation that summarizes and clarifies all the former scriptures. All the books of revelation have come down from a heavenly original that is referred to as the "guarded tablet."

The historical narratives in the biblical Scriptures present special challenges, because they are so different from the Qur'an, which is instructional rather than narrative. Although the Qur'an supports the authenticity of the biblical Scriptures, a widely held belief among Muslims is that the biblical Scriptures have been altered. How else can one account for the weaving together of narrative and instruction in the Bible?

Muslims do have their history of Muhammad, but the historical dimension is not the content of the Qur'an. The historical tomes are referred to as *hadith,* or "the Traditions." The *hadith* are texts about Muhammad that his companions collected and assembled over a span of two centuries after his death. The *hadith* are not considered to be revealed scriptures. They are accounts of what Muhammad said, did, and approved.

When Muslims read the Bible, it seems to them to be a mixture of scripture and traditions. Nevertheless, there is also curiosity about the Bible because it contains accounts of prophets the Qur'an refers to but about whom it does not present the full narrative. For example, the Qur'an refers to Joseph with some sketchy and intriguing reference to the story. However, the Bible records the narrative in full and interesting detail. It is therefore not surprising that many Muslims are quite interested in the biblical narratives. (See chapter 7 for more comments on the Muslim question about the "corruption" of biblical Scripture. Appendix C has a listing of references from the Qur'an in regard to the Bible.)

4. *Belief in angels.* This pillar is essential to the Muslim understanding of revelation. This is because Muslims believe God sent Islam down to Muhammad through the mediation of angels. Islam is communicated in the Arabic Qur'an as the revealed Word of God. The Qur'an as "sent-down" revelation is referred to as *tanzil.*

5. *Belief in the final judgment.* Muslims believe there is a balance scales. Righteous living and the performance of the duties of Islam go on the positive side of the scales. Wrongdoing and neglecting Islamic duties go onto the negative side of the scales. The final judgment is described as a time of tremendous fear as all humanity stands, awaiting the final verdict given by God himself. The verdict determines either heaven or hell as one's destiny. For some, hell will be a short-lived punishment with eventual admission into one of the levels of paradise. For others, hell may be eternal. The performance of Muslim duties is preeminently the passion to avoid the sufferings of hell. My straightforward comments on this pillar need to be balanced by the reality that there is enormous debate among Muslims with regard to judgment and reward.

6. *Predestination.* This final pillar of belief is not always mentioned by Muslims, but it is a significant dimension of Sunni Muslim faith and practice. This is the conviction that God in his sovereignty determines all that happens. This pillar of belief has invited enormous theological controversy. How does one make space for freedom of choice within a theology of the encompassing sovereignty of God? This pillar is not always mentioned, partly because there is so much debate within Islam in regard to the issues of free will and divine sovereignty.

The six pillars of duty

1. *The confession of faith.* There is no God but Allah, and Muhammad is the prophet of Allah. A person who makes that confession with intention in the presence of two male Muslim witnesses is a Muslim.

2. *The requirements of ritual prayer.* This prayer is offered five times daily. The worshiper faces Mecca as she or he bows before God. The content of the prayer is encompassed in the *Fatiha*, which is the opening *surah* of the Qur'an. The *Fatiha* is repeated a total of seventeen times daily, for it is repeated several times within each of the five daily periods of prayer. There is sometimes minor variation in the number of times the *Fatiha* prayer is repeated. Performing the prayers, including ablutions, takes about an hour a day.
3. *Giving alms for the poor.* This is an act of generosity on behalf of those who are in poverty.
4. *Fasting during the month of Ramadan.* The fast is during the daytime. At night there is feasting. Ramadan is the month when Muslims believe the revelation of the Qur'an first began. Revelation is about self-discipline; revelation is also about celebration. So the rhythm of fasting and feasting during Ramadan is a remembrance of the gift of revelation.
5. *Taking the pilgrimage to Mecca.* Every Muslim who is capable of making the pilgrimage should do so once in his or her lifetime. The saga of Ishmael and Hagar looking for water when they were sent from the home of Abraham is reenacted during the pilgrimage. Thousands of animals are sacrificed to remember Ishmael who, as they believe, was redeemed from death by God's provision of a tremendous substitute sacrifice.
6. *Jihad, or striving in the way of God.* Jihad is a commitment to preserving the integrity of the house of Islam. There are two forms of jihad: the lesser and the greater. The greater jihad is the jihad of the soul—striving to be a sincere Muslim whose outer and inner commitment is united. The lesser jihad is defending the house of Islam in any way necessary when it is under threat. The lesser jihad can have several expressions. First is the jihad of the pen or mouth, which is defending Islam apologetically. The second is the use of the sword as a last resort when all other attempts to protect the house of Islam have failed.

This simple construct—six pillars of duty and six of belief—unites the house of Islam around the world. All Muslims who are acquainted with and committed to Islam will embrace these pillars. They define Muslim theology, worldview, and commitments. *Tauhid* is the integration of these twelve pillars within the *umma*, bringing all areas of life under the authority of God.

After observing a Muslim friend in prayer, I asked, "Does it get wearisome investing an hour a day as you prostrate thirty-four times daily and confess the *Fatiha* seventeen times?"

This man was a busy man; he was a surgeon. Enthusiastically he responded, "As I bow in prayer, I feel washed by the will of God. When I think of God my creator, then an hour of prayer a day is not adequate to express my gratitude."

In the five times of daily prayer, the worldwide Muslim *umma* turns toward the same center: the black stone in Mecca encompassed by a structure known as the *Ka'bah*. All Muslims bow toward the *Ka'bah* in their required prostrations.

Professor Amir, a visiting Muslim scholar in the United States, describes the significance of the black stone of the *Ka'bah*: "It was thought to be a holy stone that came from heaven to show Adam and Eve where to make an altar. Then it was part of the *Ka'aba* Abraham built, and after Islam the generation of it continued. The main thing is that it is symbolically taken to invoke a sense of holiness and reference to Allah as it is part of the house of God, the *Ka'aba*."[1]

Brief comparison between the *umma* and the church

Once, when speaking about the house of Islam to a Christian gathering, I asked, "Is there anything you wish you could offer this house?" A girl, probably twelve years old, raised her hand and said, "Salvation. There is no salvation in that house."

Muslims would most likely agree with her. Some years ago when I was writing *A Muslim and a Christian in Dialogue* with Badru Kateregga, I suggested he write a chapter on salvation in Islam. He declined, saying that in Islam there is no concept of salvation as in the gospel understanding of salvation. He explained

---

1. Professor Seyed Amir Akrami, visiting Muslim scholar at Eastern Mennonite University, email message to author, June 13, 2014.

that Islam is instruction on what one should believe and how one should act. Islam gives instruction on the pillars of support for the house of Islam. Islam is not about salvation, but rather about instruction.

So my colleague wrote a chapter on the peace of submission to the will of God. He explained that in Islam, God might offer paradise to those who submit to God's will, but God does not come down to save us and redeem us. As I listen to Muslims, it is clear that they yearn for an eternal reward given by God, their compassionate creator. Islam is the instruction on how to conduct themselves as they journey toward the final judgment.

The church is referred to as the temple of the living God. The church is not an edifice in the sense we are describing. Rather, the church is the people for whom Jesus the Messiah is the center. The church is a community of people redeemed through the grace of God revealed in Jesus the Messiah.

The great city: the church

The book of Revelation, the concluding Scripture of the Bible, contains some surprising metaphors for the house of God—namely, the church.[2] The church is described as the great and beautiful city that comes down from heaven. It is called "the bride of the Lamb [Christ]." This metaphor suggests a joyous and loving relationship. The description of the church as the city from heaven means the church is God's creation; it comes from heaven. However, all the materials in the city are from earth. Here is a vision of God and those who believe working together to form the city of God. (I am using both *the city of God* and *the church* to describe the community of believers committed to Jesus the Messiah. See note 3 in chapter 2.)

The twelve gates

The city is surrounded by twelve gates that are grand pearls. Those gates are the twelve tribes of Israel, and the gates are always open; all peoples are welcome. All of this began with the call of Abraham. God called Abraham to leave the world of his

---

2. Bible: Revelation 21.

people who were ensnared in polytheistic practices. God promised that through Abraham's seed, all nations would be blessed. Abraham's grandson Jacob (later known as Israel) had twelve sons. Each of those sons became a tribe in Israel. Theirs was a tumultuous story of ups and downs, faithfulness and failure. In the midst of it all, God was at work preparing the nations to receive his gift of salvation, which would be fulfilled by the appearance of the promised Messiah.

We have already mentioned that the Qur'an reveals an appreciation for the biblical Scriptures. Muslims believe they should respect all the prophets of God and all scripture, including the Old Testament Scriptures. There is more written about Moses in the Qur'an than any other prophet. Muhammad had a keen hope that his mission would be understood as in continuity with the prophets of Israel. The modern Muslim conflict with Israel, beginning already at the time of Muhammad, often obscures the significance of the prophets and scriptures that have come to us through Israel.

For example, it is through God's revelation to the prophet Moses that humankind first heard the astonishing news: "In the beginning God created the heavens and the earth."[3] The significance of these prophets and scriptures is recognized in the Qur'an and especially in *surah* 17, called The Children of Israel (*Bani Israil*).

The twelve foundation stones

The city from heaven also has twelve foundation stones. These stones are the twelve apostles. Each is a precious gem; each apostle contributes his special gift.[4] It is the apostolic witness, and especially the writings, that have provided the firm foundation for the church.

Muslims proclaim the twelve pillars supporting the house of Islam: six of duty and six of belief. The city of God as described in Revelation is formed by twelve gates and twelve foundation stones. The gates are the way into the city, and those gates are always open. They invite the nations and the kings to come! The

3. Bible: Genesis 1:1.
4. Bible: Revelation 21:14, 19-20.

city is eternal; it is securely built upon the life and witness of the twelve apostles.

The Lamb in the center of the church

We have observed that Muslims believe the will of God, as revealed in the Qur'an, is at the center of the *umma*. At the center of the church, as revealed in the book of Revelation, we meet a wounded lamb—standing! Jesus is called the Lamb of God. The wounded lamb that is standing means Jesus Christ crucified and risen is in the center of the church.

The church meets the *umma*

Sometimes I am surprised by the invitations to participate in the meeting of church and *umma*. With their different centers, the church and *umma* certainly contain areas of convergence and divergence. That was my experience in Tehran, Iran, several years ago. A letter came across my desk announcing a gathering in Tehran for an international conference on Mahdism. The letter was accompanied by an invitation for papers. One presentation was called "Messianic Hope in Abrahamic Religions." I wrote back, saying I would like to present on Messianic hope in the Christian faith. The organizers invited me to speak; as it turned out two other Christians also made presentations.

Iran is Shi'ite Muslim. Their branch of Shi'ite theology teaches that the twelfth imam, who was a descendant of Muhammad's daughter Fatima, vanished. He is known as Mahdi (a savior figure). These Shi'ites believe the Mahdi will return with Jesus to spread Islam to the whole world. His return will happen when Iranian society has become faithful to Islam. That is what the Iranian Islamic Revolution is about: developing faithful obedience to Islam in preparation for the coming of Jesus and the Mahdi.

At least two thousand clerics from around the world gathered in the rotunda in central Tehran. In the foyer a video loop was saying, "Jesus is coming soon with the Mahdi; are you ready?" During the conference I heard twenty-one sermons on Mahdism! The longest sermon was by Iranian president Mahmoud Ahmadinejad. He interwove Mahdism and the state of the world.

I spoke with Ahmadinejad briefly, inviting him to participate in the future in a dialogue with North American church leaders. That happened. When I took the podium I asked all to wave their hands who wished to send greetings to churches I visit around the world. I nearly wept at the sight of a couple thousand turbaned Shi'ite clergy from around the world waving their greetings to churches around the world.

I spoke for twenty minutes. I thanked them for inviting me. I said I would speak about the gospel. I spoke of the life of Jesus, beginning with his virgin birth. I began my message with the first sermon Jesus preached in his home synagogue in Nazareth. That was my foundation theme: "Today this scripture is fulfilled in your hearing."[5] I spoke of his life, teachings, crucifixion, resurrection, and commission.

Then the moderator firmly intoned, "Your time is up!"

I concluded with an excerpt from the Lord's Prayer: "[May] your kingdom come, [may] your will be done, on earth as it is in heaven."[6]

Back in my seat I quickly grasped the headset.

The chairperson was saying, "We did not know this about Jesus. We must investigate what Shenk has shared with us. My message to you Christians is to make your books available for us to commence the study."

Of course, all the books I had referred to were biblical texts. My soul was filled with gratitude at this affirming response.

Surprised by women

Several women addressed this assembly of clerics. I was surprised, for my caricature was that in Iran women are repressed. These women were either PhDs or pursuing higher education. They had lucid, forceful, and creative presentations that seemed well received.

A couple of years later I was participating in another dialogue in an academic venue in North America. This was an Iranian-North American conversation. A dozen Iranian women were accompanying clerics and other scholars. The event focused on similarities and differences in Muslim and Christian anthropology. After

---

5. Bible: Luke 4:18-21.
6. Bible: Matthew 6:10.

the formal dialogue, the women entered a course on Christian approaches to peacemaking taught by a Christian university. I understood that this exchange was orchestrated by one of the theological training centers in Iran.

I share these episodes as a challenge to our caricatures of the role of women in Muslim societies. There is obviously a lot of diversity! As we consider social transformations that enhance the role of women in both Muslim and Western societies, we do well to be in touch with the transforming currents that are flowing in many Muslim societies.

Communities of healing for the nations

In the concluding paragraphs of the Bible we have seen that the city of God brings healing to the nations. We also read that the Lamb standing in the city is light to the nations. I will explore briefly what it means for the church to be a community of healing among the nations and a light to the nations. I will also give special attention to the relationship of the church to the *umma*.

Jesus promised that when two or more meet in his name, there he is in the midst.[7] The two or three is significant. In many regions of the Muslim world, the church is literally only two or three. In some regions there are numerous believers, but often they are few.

Jesus is the light within that circle of believers, whether few or many. He is the crucified and risen Messiah standing in the midst of the city. He is providing the light for the city. He is also providing light for the nations. We meet the nations coming into his light. We meet the redeemed who have repented and whose names are in the Lamb's book of life; we meet them streaming into the city.

What does this mean: the nations walking by the light of the city of God and the kings bringing their honor into the city? A reflection on the Middle East might help explain. Some years ago, two of my acquaintances met with the late King Hussein of Jordan. He told them the churches in the Middle East were the only hope for the region, because the churches were the only communities committed to authentic reconciliation.

7. Bible: Matthew 18:20.

About the time of this meeting, Bishop Elias Chacour in Galilee had written a book on reconciliation entitled *Blood Brothers*.[8] The king commented that he had personally bought five thousand copies of the book and sent these to his family, all members of his government, and every political leader across the Middle East. The reconciliation and forgiveness the bishop was describing was a healing witness desperately needed, Hussein said.

Around the world we discover the faithful church, which welcomes the presence of the Lamb in their midst and becomes a community of healing and grace. Surely that is what is meant by describing Jesus as the light of the city and the light who shows the way for nations.

Healing for the person

Jesus the Messiah is not only the healer of the nations; he is also the healer of the person. I am emphasizing the community and national dimensions of the healing peace of Jesus in this book, mostly because our current geopolitical realities in Christian-Muslim relations are so challenged. However, it is equally important to recognize the healing grace of Jesus for the person.

Only a month ago, Grace and I visited in a country where it is unconstitutional for a person to become a Christian. We met a person who, at risk to her life, had committed to the Messiah. Why did she do that? She told us it is because Jesus the Messiah found her, and she has found in him eternal salvation. She explained that in the Messiah she has been touched with peace and healing for her soul. We hear those stories around the world. People come to Jesus, for he is the healer of the person.

Sociologist Philip Jenkins has written numerous books on the global church. After the publication of one of his books on the Christian faith in the Global South, I heard him being interviewed on National Public Radio. The interviewer asked, "Professor Jenkins, how do you account for the spread of the church through the Global South?"

He replied, "Jesus. It is because of Jesus that the church is spreading. Jesus is the healer—not necessarily physical

---

8. Elias Chacour with David Hazard, *Blood Brothers* (Grand Rapids, MI: Zondervan, 1984).

healing—but he is the healer of the person." I believe the professor got that right!

A life-giving river
In the description of the city we also meet the river of life.[9] The river comes from the throne of God and from the Lamb. The river is the Holy Spirit flowing through the street of the city, bringing forth the tree of life, which has fruit for every season and leaves for the healing of the nations. What an amazing river! The fruit from the tree is the fruit of the Holy Spirit: love, joy, peace, patience, kindness, goodness, faithfulness, gentleness, and self-control.[10] The leaves of healing are righteous people who, through their righteous ways, are transforming their communities and nations for good.

The church has a special responsibility to be a community of reconciliation. The church is the only community on earth that believes Jesus the Messiah, crucified and risen, is in the center of God's grand plan for the healing of the nations. It is within the church that the good news is proclaimed: God is love. The gates are always open. All are welcome!

Questions for discussion
1. What is the mission of each of the three Abrahamic faiths? Each of these faiths believes that God reveals truth. What is the center of revelation for each of the three Abrahamic faiths?
2. Describe the six pillars of belief and six pillars of duty that support the house of Islam.
3. Describe the twelve gates and twelve foundation stones that compose New Jerusalem (the church).[11]
4. What is the significance for Muslims of bowing toward Mecca in prayer?
5. The Lamb is at the center of New Jerusalem.[12] What is the significance of the Lamb in the center of the church?

---

9. Bible: Revelation 22:1-4.
10. Bible: Galatians 5:22-23.
11. Bible: Revelation 21:12-15.
12. Bible: Revelation 5:6; 21:22-23; 22:1.

CHAPTER 6

Practice Hospitality

The eternally open gates of the city of God as described in Revelation remind me of the hospitality in the home of an African pastoral colleague in Nairobi. He told me that when he was a boy living in a rural area of Kenya, his father would step outside their home at mealtime and look into the distance. He was checking to see if there was any stranger walking the footpath beyond their home.

If his father saw a stranger, he would lift his voice in a mighty call: "Ho! It is dinnertime! Come to my house and eat!" This is the spirit of hospitality we meet in these Revelation verses describing the city from heaven.

The house of Islam also has open doors. All are welcome. Five times a day, from minarets around the world, the invitation goes forth to receive the hospitality of community and worship. The Muslim witness and invitation is clear: God is most great. I bear witness that Muhammad is the prophet of God, so come and receive well-being. Come and pray.

As I have done above, it is helpful to compare the house of Islam and the city of God as described in the book of Revelation. Viewing these different communities as congregations of invitation is helpful. Knowing what people are being invited into is also important. However, for the remainder of the book I will usually use the term *umma* when referring to the house of Islam and *church* when referring to the believers in Jesus the Messiah.

Communities of hospitality

Both the faithful church and the faithful Muslim *umma* are communities of hospitality. In fact, the Qur'an encourages Muslims
to compete with Christians in extending hospitality and good
deeds. The Qur'an also observes Christians are people of compassionate hearts.[1] Christians and Muslims are encouraged to
feast together.[2] The Qur'an lauds sacrificial generosity:

> It is not righteousness that you turn your faces toward
> East or West; but it is righteousness—to believe in Allah
> and the Last Day, and the Angels, and the Book, and the
> Messengers; to spend of your substance, out of love for
> Him, for your kin, for orphans, for the needy, for the way-
> farer, for those who ask, and for the ransom of slaves;
> to be steadfast in prayer, and practice regular charity;
> to fulfill the contracts which you have made; and to be
> firm and patient, in pain (or suffering) and adversity and
> throughout all periods of panic. Such are the people of
> truth, those who fear Allah.[3]

This is a call to generosity indeed! We have often experienced
expressions of extravagant generosity from Muslims, as described
in these spiritual and ethical teachings of the Qur'an.

Some years ago when in Somalia, I went to the home of one
of the students in our school. We drove, which was an indica-
tion of our immense wealth in comparison to the poor village he
came from. As we sat in his home, his mother took a couple of
pennies from her dress and sent a child to buy a tiny pouch of
red sweetener, which she placed in a pot of river water for their
honored guest. I knew the water was dangerous for my system. I
reminded the Lord that he promised we could handle snakes, and
so I drank the most extravagant gift this dear woman could offer.

Shortly after completing college, one of our sons invested
over half a year traveling in the Middle East. Those travels cost
him almost nothing; local hospitality carried him along. During
three weeks in Algeria his costs were fully covered by those who

---

1. Qur'an: *Hadid* (Iron): surah 57:27.
2. Qur'an: *Maida* (The Table Spread): surah 5:5.
3. Qur'an: *Baqara* (The Heifer): surah 2:177.

offered him hospitality, including people as diverse as truck drivers and even a Muslim sultan. When he got to the Algerian border the agents were not pleased he had spent so little money; for a moment it seemed they would send him back into the desert to spend some cash!

Our father was hospitable!

Indeed, we have often experienced Muslim hospitality. But Christians are not exempt from the call to be hospitable. A conversation I had several years ago is pertinent, as an account of Christian hospitality extended to refugees, most of whom were Muslims. I was writing the memoir of Ahmed Ali Haile, a Somali disciple of Jesus the Messiah. I asked his teenage children what should be especially mentioned. They squirmed a bit, and their father said jovially, "You aren't speaking because you want to report your father is a dictator, but you are too kind to say that."

"Oh, no!" they exclaimed. "Dad is not a dictator! This is what you must say. Dad was committed to hospitality. If a Somali refugee appeared at our home at two o'clock in the morning, Dad would give them a place to sleep. Guests were always at our table. Dad was hospitable, and all our family got into the spirit of generous hospitality. The hospitality of our home was a very strong witness to the love of the Messiah."

I pressed the point. "But your father's hospitality meant sometimes you needed to get out of bed at two in the morning and give your bed to a refugee you did not know, while you slept on the floor."

"Yes, that is true. But we must realize hospitality is welcoming the stranger even when it is not convenient."

This family bought one hundred pounds of sugar for tea for guests each month! Most guests would put five spoonfuls of sugar in their tea, so that explains a little of the volume, but not much. Guests were almost always at their table for meals. This was a family with open hearts for all who would stop by. Their legacy is a remarkable statement of loving care for the refugee and oppressed.

My one deep regret about our six years in Nairobi is that we did not ourselves give with sufficient generosity for the enormous

Somali refugee situation. We too easily felt the situation was beyond us, and so did very little. We also were quite concerned
about government authorities who were not favorable to assist-
ing refugees. However, we should have done more. I grieve about
that, and have asked a number of Somalis their forgiveness. My
friend whose memoir I helped write has opened my heart to a
more generous spirit.

A cup of cold water

Jesus promised a blessing to those who give a cup of cold water
in his name.[4] We experienced that blessing. Although we did not
marshal resources such as food to help in the refugee crisis, our
home was always open. Grace kept bananas and bread on our
kitchen shelf for any hungry people who knocked on our door.
Living in a highly congested area of Nairobi, we had the only
phone on the block, so our living room became an occasional
phone center. In the five-apartment complex in Eastleigh where
we stayed, we reserved one apartment for homeless Somali fellows. Lots of people stopped in, and Grace's culinary gifts were
much appreciated.

The children also contributed to the spirit of hospitality. Our
family had a good relationship with the imam in the mosque and
with his family. Our girls became best friends of his daughters,
and when he became ill, I was invited into his home to pray for his
healing. Our sons learned the fast foot moves of street soccer by
playing with youth from the mosque and the church. In remarkable ways, our children facilitated our blending into Eastleigh.

After six years in Nairobi, when our time had come to leave
Kenya, friends and colleagues gave farewell events and speeches.
I had worked in the university, written books, and given leadership to several programs. Those accomplishments were barely
mentioned in the farewell statements, however. What we heard
was appreciation for hospitality. People observed, "Grace always
had a cup of cold water or hot tea ready for any who stopped in."
As I listened, it became clear to me that those gracious expressions of hospitality given by Grace and our children were a most
significant dimension of our ministry.

---

4. Bible: Mark 9:41.

Language: the challenge of hospitality

Language is a profound reality when extending and receiving hospitality. Let me illustrate. For many years Christian friends went with me regularly to the mosque on the Islamic Way in Baltimore. This mosque was planted by an African American who, after his conversion to Islam, went to Saudi Arabia for ten years for immersion in Arabic and Islamic studies. As an imam, he knew that the study of Arabic was important, because Muslims believe the Qur'an was sent down to Muhammad in the Arabic language. Shortly after the imam's return to Baltimore, I was in the mosque one evening when an old man walked in from the street.

He wandered to the front where we were sitting with the imam and said, "I want to be a Muslim!" The congregation erupted with reverent praises to God. Then the imam said that he must repeat in Arabic the confession of faith: there is no God but Allah, and Muhammad is the prophet of God. After he repeated the confession, the imam stated, "Now you are a Muslim. And there is an obligation. The required prayers are in Arabic, and so is the Qur'an. So you must learn Arabic. Before you leave this evening, register for Arabic classes here in the mosque."

The drama in the mosque that evening—providing Arabic classes for the elderly convert to Islam—was a window into the global *umma*. As the *umma* grows into communities around the world, it takes the Arabic language with it. Islamization and Arabization are complementary realities.

That reality was evident another evening at the same mosque. About a year later I was back in that mosque and met an imam from Saudi Arabia sitting beside the local imam. When we asked questions, the local imam who had established this mosque would say, "I will defer the question to our brother from Arabia, because he knows Arabic better than I do!" Not only was the mosque in Baltimore becoming an Arabic training center, but the authority of the local mosque was shifting toward those who knew Arabic best. It is those most proficient in Arabic who are likely the most capable teachers of Islam.

Contrast these exchanges in the mosque with my recent experience in my childhood church among the Zanaki people in Tanzania. Between choirs singing, an old woman in her nineties, bowed over with arthritis, stood up during the service and held high a Zanaki translation of the gospel of Matthew. She sang, "This books tells all about Jesus—this book tells all about salvation! Believe the message of this book!"

She was worshiping and singing in her mother tongue! It felt like Pentecost on the birthday of the church in Jerusalem. At Pentecost when the church was formed, people from "every nation under heaven" heard the gospel proclaimed in their own language: Parthians, Medes, and Elamites; people from Mesopotamia, Judea, Cappadocia, Pontus, Asia, Phrygia, Pamphylia, Egypt, Libya, and Rome; Cretans and Arabs.[5]

The Word of God in the language of people around the world is a gift of cultural and linguistic hospitality that the Muslim *umma* cannot duplicate. One of the attractions of the Christian faith is the conviction that God makes no language boundaries or requirements. The church invites people from all languages to worship at the table in their mother tongue!

Extending and receiving hospitality

This does not mean Muslims are not hospitable. In fact, in the mosque in Baltimore we were sometimes served an ample meal as we intermingled with the congregation. The Qur'an is explicit in its command: Muslims and Christians should extend hospitality to one another. Muslims like to recall two stories from early in the Muslim movement. We have already mentioned the first account, when the Christians of Ethiopia extended hospitality to the persecuted Muslims from Mecca.

Equally significant is a visit of Christians from Yemen to Muhammad. He gave them access to the Muslim mosque in Medina for their prayers and a place to find refreshment from their journey. In that spirit Muslims are encouraged to extend and receive hospitality to Christians.[6]

A common word

The hospitality modeled in this visit was commended recently in a surprising letter sent by Muslims to the worldwide Christian

---

5. Bible: Acts 2:5-12.
6. Alfred Guillaume, *The Life of Muhammad* (Pakistan: Oxford University Press, 1967), 270–77.

church. It is dated October 13, 2007. This is probably the first time a worldwide representation of Muslims addressed a letter to all Christians. The premise was that Muslims and Christians, because they represent half the world's population, carry a special responsibility for world peace. The letter urged that a starting point can be love of God and love of neighbor.[7] The writers stated those two commandments are embedded as core commitments both in the Torah and in the *Injil* (gospel). The letter is long—about forty pages.[8]

Not surprisingly, the letter, titled "A Common Word," elicited varied and sometimes passionate responses. Some felt this was a bold Muslim attempt to subvert the gospel; others felt this was one of the most amazing developments in the history of Christian-Muslim relations. At least one person is writing his PhD dissertation about "A Common Word."

In this short book, I cannot address the implications. However, I was delighted to be invited into several forums where the letter was discussed. In one forum the Muslim representatives from Mecca said they hoped to invite me to come to Mecca and share the Christian understanding of the trinity of God! They said that since my name is David and I believe in one God, they hoped they could get an invitation for me. That has not happened yet, but it illustrates some of the open doors for conversations and bearing witness that these forums provided in the wake of the release of this letter. Many Muslims and Christians had never before experienced the kind of heart-to-heart dialogue these forums provided. (Appendix D of this book offers one Mennonite group's response.)

Protocols of Muslims and Christians eating together

Of course, there must be respectful protocols for such experiences.[9] It is mandatory for Christians who are inviting Muslims

---

7. Bible: Mark 12:29-32.

8. The full text of "A Common Word between Us and You" is available at the letter's official website www.acommonword.com. The Mennonite Church USA response to "A Common Word" appears as appendix D.

9. Bruce A. McDowell and Anees Zaka, *Muslims and Christians at the Table: Promoting Biblical Understanding among North American Muslims* (Phillipsburg, NJ: P&R Publishing, 1999), 171–216. This book has helpful suggestions for extending and receiving hospitality with Muslims.

for a meal to acquire *halal* (lawful and permitted in Islam) food. Most communities have a *halal* grocery where meats have been prepared in accordance to Muslim requirements. If there are no *halal* meats available in your community, then have a vegetarian meal. Assure your Muslim guests that either the meat is *halal* or they will be served a vegetarian meal. Protocol will insist the plates and utensils you use have not touched pork or other prohibited foods. The Muslim guest will appreciate being assured by her Christian hosts that they have been sensitive to these concerns.

When invited into a Muslim home, some Christians will hesitate to eat meat that has been prepared in accordance with Muslim protocols, which include the invocation of the name of God as the animal is killed. In my judgment, Paul's counsel to the Corinthians is helpful. He advises we should receive all food with thanksgiving in the name of Christ, who makes all foods clean.[10] The hospitality of eating together is a wonderful and helpful step in nurturing friendship and trust. I think of hospitality as this: those who dwell in the house of Islam and those who dwell in the city of God visiting back and forth.

Welcome Muslim guests

Muslims are usually delighted to be invited into a Christian home. That was the experience of friends of ours, who tell of the day they invited a Muslim neighbor family to their home for dinner. The family appeared dressed in their finest clothing; they were obviously excited. As it turned out, they had lived in the United States for about thirty years, and this was the first time a Christian family had invited them to their home for dinner. It was a marvelous evening!

Recently my wife and I hosted a Shi'ite family in our home. The family included two teenage daughters. As soon as they arrived they rather urgently informed us it was the time for prayer. They needed to know the exact direction of Mecca, which we did not know. So they set up their computer to get a fix on Mecca, and we provided a room for prayers. That evening we had a remarkable conversation, some of it centered on faith questions.

---

10. Bible: 1 Corinthians 10:23-27.

Then the next morning they joined us for our regular morning worship together, including the Bible reading. We sang a song entitled "I Owe the Lord a Morning Song." They appreciated our time of worship at the beginning of the day, and they invited us to Iran, promising to host us in their home.

Community-to-community hospitality

Recently several local churches in our community and a large mosque congregation joined hands for a hospitality weekend. This included a feast together. Probably the best part of the event was listening to one another's faith stories and hearing some of the challenges as followers of God in the United States. A small team has been appointed to explore further ways of extending hospitality. The Christians are clear that they are believers in Jesus and seek to live within the hospitality and invitation God extends to us in the life and mission of the Messiah. The mostly immigrant Muslims cherish the opportunity to broaden their circles of friendship. One step the two communities are taking is developing Arabic classes for the immigrant children, because parents fear their children might lose their Arabic as they become more comfortable with English.

In both Somalia and Nairobi, we made the most of Christmas. Muslims have only a modest celebration of the birth of Muhammad. The Ramadan breaking of the fast and the Feast of Sacrifice at the time of the annual pilgrimage are more celebrative than remembrance of Muhammad's birth. Nevertheless, the birth of the Messiah is a good time to invite neighbors for a celebration. In Somalia and Nairobi, the small believing community would arrange for killing a goat and have it prepared in the most savory way. We invited many Muslim friends. Wonderful music filled the air, much of it songs about Jesus, whose birth we were celebrating. Then in Somalia we usually had a dramatic rendition of the Christmas story. If we did not have a pageant, we would tell the Christmas story.

Occasionally we receive Christmas cards from Muslims; surely they in turn would appreciate cards from their Christian friends. Although I have not gotten into the practice of sending cards during the Muslim holidays, occasionally during the month of the pilgrimage I write to Muslim friends saying I am praying for the pilgrims. I pray for their safety; sometimes tragedies befall the pilgrims. I also pray for revelations of truth as they take their journey.

As we have mentioned, Somalia was restrictive. We usually informed local authorities of our plan to have an appropriate Christmas celebration. We assured them there would be no alcohol. By keeping the authorities informed, we hoped there would be no disturbances. We never had any objections to the event, and much expression of appreciation.

A United Nations officer and his wife from South India would invite the Somali government officers he worked with to a Christmas Eve party. It consisted of listening to the entire rendition of Handel's *Messiah*, followed by delicacies and joyful conversations. Their family always received heartfelt thanks from the Somali representatives. It is amazing how extending hospitality can open doors we might otherwise consider closed.

In summary, the Qur'an encourages Muslims to cultivate a collegial and generous spirit toward guests. In fact, Muslims are to compete in extending hospitality.[11] In many communities Muslims and Christians enjoy sharing with one another in their festivals, Christians inviting Muslims to their feasts and Muslims inviting Christians to theirs.

Cautions about friendship

While it is true the Qur'an encourages reciprocal hospitality between the *umma* and the church, there are also warnings about possible dangers emerging out of the goodwill nurtured by hospitality. The concern lurking around the corner is that hospitality and friendship might seduce a Muslim away from Islam into the Christian faith. In that case the Qur'an is forthright; the friendship must end.[12]

Furthermore, if perchance hospitality were to fan the embers of romance between a Christian man and a Muslim woman, the friendship must end, unless the man converts to Islam. However, a romantic friendship between a Muslim man and a Christian

---

11. Qur'an: *Nisaa* (Women): surah 4:86.
12. Qur'an: *Baqara* (The Heifer): surah 2:109; *Ali Imran* (The Family of Imran): surah 3:69.

woman is allowed; the children will belong to the man and he will raise them Muslim. These realities mean it is not wise for a Muslim and a Christian to become romantically involved. This is the position Paul took in his letter to the Corinthians, writing about similar issues in Corinth.[13] His admonition certainly also applies to Christian-Muslim relations.

Christians have the same concerns about the use of hospitality as a tool for evangelism. If a Muslim fellow would befriend one of my grandchildren and then invite her to the mosque, I would have concerns. I do not view the Muslim cautions as adversarial. Rather, they are understandable concerns, if indeed the Muslim holds the Muslim faith as a treasure, as I do my commitment to Christ.

Relating to Muslim neighbors

When teaching a course on faithful Christian witness among Muslims in an African country, I assigned the students to meet with a Muslim neighbor. They were to ask one question: What suggestions do you have for building peaceful relations between Muslims and Christians?

The class almost rebelled. They feared the Muslims would attack them. It was clear some steps at relationship building were urgently needed. So I made the assignment voluntary with the promise of additional credit. As I recall, only three out of a class of thirty ultimately decided not to undertake the assignment. Those who did the assignment were thrilled by the responses. The Muslims were keen about these Christians caring enough to ask such a question. All the Muslims had enthusiastic suggestions. Only one suggestion was deemed inadvisable by the class: that was for Christian women to marry Muslim men.

Occasionally I get a phone call about how to develop trusting relations with Muslim colleagues. Recently someone asked, "David, a Muslim neighbor has moved in next door. What is your advice?"

Welcome the family to your neighborhood and become acquainted. Foremost is learning about your new neighbors. Discern whether they have concerns about their neighborhood. Do what

---

13. Bible: 2 Corinthians 6:14-15.

you can to help them settle into their new routines. Before long, invite them to your home for a welcome dinner. Assure them the food will be vegetarian, or if meat, *halal*. Enjoy the evening.

As we have mentioned in these chapters, most Muslims appreciate conversations about God. Most likely, at some time your neighbors will ask about your faith and church. It is likely that at some time they would appreciate receiving a Bible from you, as a friend giving them a special autographed gift. They might appreciate joining you in a walk through the Bible. Many Muslims are intrigued by the Bible narratives and the message of salvation. Nurture the relationship!

My best friend in our neighborhood is a Muslim. I cherish the times we have had over a cup of coffee or eating breakfast together!

Political implications of hospitality

I have mentioned two events during the time of Muhammad that are charming examples of hospitality. The first was when three hundred Muslims from Mecca migrated to Christian Ethiopia. They fled from Mecca to receive protection from harassment in Mecca. The other event occurred when Christians from Yemen were welcomed into the mosque in Medina, where they could be refreshed and have a Christian worship service. These two events are often mentioned by modern Muslims as examples of ideal Christian-Muslim relations. But there is political significance of such generous hospitality too.

For example, Switzerland has extended hospitality to thousands of Muslims who are refugees from their Muslim homelands. This is generous and right. Then comes a special challenge. The Muslim refugees want to build mosques with minarets. These concerns were addressed in a referendum wherein the Swiss determined that they would not permit minarets in Switzerland; however, mosques are permitted.

How far should Christians extend hospitality to Muslims? In Great Britain, the Anglican Archbishop of Canterbury has indicated that the church should support the Muslim quest to live under Islamic Shari'a law, at least for domestic matters. That has attracted vigorous debate. For example, does this mean polygamy (which is sanctioned in Islamic Shari'a law) should be countenanced for Muslims in Great Britain?

France draws the line forthrightly by asserting that France is unapologetically secular. Muslim girls and women are prohibited from wearing the *hijab* in government buildings or schools; however, they may wear it in public. Nevertheless, the *niqab*, which covers the face, is not permitted in public. For many Muslims, those restrictions seem to be a violation of religious freedom.

In contrast, Canada has an intentional policy of encouraging multiculturalism. Yet, even in Canada there are expectations that Muslims will abide by certain norms the Christianized or secularized society upholds. For example, in Islam, the children belong to the father in the case of divorce; in Canada, the judge determines who has primary care of the children.

How should the spirit of hospitality guide Christian-Muslim relations within the challenges of sometimes very different values? We need to find the way. It is one thing to invite Muslim neighbors over for a Sunday afternoon tea together. In some places it has become quite another matter if Muslims wish to build a minaret!

Discussion about core values

In these discussions, I do not recommend a relativistic approach to values. One reason Muslims search for ways to immigrate to the West is their appreciation for Western Christianized values. Those values should not be squandered; they are a gift we should not abandon.

That issue was the essence of a heated debate several years ago in a conversation riding in a packed car from London to Heathrow Airport. My Muslim hosts were trying to impress upon me the merits of Islamic Shari'a law for the restoration of decadent Britain. I was in vigorous rebuttal.

Then all was silent for a minute until one of my hosts exclaimed, "If we are honest, we all agree with David. We love the West and the freedoms we enjoy. That is why none of us are flying to Pakistan tonight; we are all going to Canada, for we love the Canadian ethos."

Examples of caring

On one occasion, an immigrant Muslim congregation confided to me that in their community outside Philadelphia, the churches are their most trusted allies. If they need land to build a mosque and zoning challenges arise, the churches will stand by the Muslims to defend their right to build a mosque. It is not always that way. But I was delighted to hear that this mosque experienced the churches as genuine welcoming communities.

Another Muslim congregation told me that when the World Trade Center was attacked, local pastors met with the leaders of the mosque to pledge that if any of the Muslim women needed to go shopping, a Christian woman from the churches would accompany them. That gesture of goodwill and support was enormously appreciated.

Thousands of Muslim students from around the world live in university dormitories in Canada and the United States. Most are never invited into the homes of Christian families. I have mentioned that a couple of weeks ago, a friend took some Iraqi students on an outing on the nearby Susquehanna River. The students were elated. I suppose they will never forget the joy of a Sunday afternoon on the river! Hospitality is a joy!

When I was teaching a course on Islam in Sarajevo, Bosnia, most participants in my class were formerly Muslim. I asked a participant, who was probably in her fifties, "How did you become a Christian?"

Tears trickled down her cheeks as she said, "I am a Christian because a Christian became my best friend."

Questions for discussion

1. Describe examples of hospitality that you have received. In what ways has receiving hospitality been significant for you?
2. Describe experiences of extending hospitality.
3. Imagine what it feels like to be a refugee. Are there ways you or your church could be more proactive in extending hospitality to the refugee?
4. Reflect on the mandate in the Bible and the Qur'an to practice hospitality.

CHAPTER 7

Answer the Questions

The *umma* asks the church four basic questions about the Christian faith. I experience these same questions when meeting Muslims around the world. Furthermore, when I read the early history of Christian-Muslim relations, I discover the same questions have been with us for more than a thousand years.

1. Have the Christian Scriptures been altered from the original revelation?
2. What do you mean by calling Jesus the Son of God?
3. What is the meaning of the Trinity?
4. How could the Messiah be crucified?

There is often a fifth question: what do you think of Muhammad? We have already commented on that question. The other four questions must be addressed if there is to be any credibility in bearing witness to the gospel.

Most often these are not tea parlor conversations, but rather questions coming in the most unexpected ways. As we were traveling the fifty miles in a clattery bus from Mogadishu to our home in Johar, Somalia, a passenger at the front shouted back to us above the jukebox staccato, "Who are you?" I gave him my Somali name, Daud Sheikh. "Oh," he exclaimed, "so you are a Muslim!"

"Actually, I am a follower of Jesus the Messiah!"

"So you believe God had a wife who bore him a son?"

In a situation like that, it is unwise and impossible to have a conversation. So I simply denied emphatically that God has a spouse! I invited him to meet me for further conversation.

Accept the questions

Sometimes I experience such questions as confrontational or intended to put me into a corner. Some Muslim debaters are unkind and disrespectful. However, that is unusual.

Frequently, after an evening with Muslims in a mosque, the imam will conclude by saying, "If in any way we Muslims have been unkind or offended, we ask your forgiveness."

I usually experience Muslim questions to be sincere efforts to resolve perplexities. For example, some years ago I was part of a dialogue at The Interchurch Center in Manhattan. In the middle of our searching conversations, a highly respected Muslim theologian asked, "How can you believe Jesus was crucified? That means God was unable to rescue him from the cross. That cannot be."

Six months later I was in Bangladesh, chatting in the evening with illiterate peasants. They asked me, "How can you believe Jesus was crucified? That is impossible, for God is all powerful and would never let the Messiah be crucified."

Twelve thousand miles apart, one conversation with highly educated theologians and the other with illiterate peasants—but the same question expressed with sincerity and perplexity.

Has the Bible been changed?

Usually the first question is about the Bible. For many Muslims, the idea that the biblical texts have been "corrupted" seems the only way to resolve their perplexity about the Bible. So it is important to keep in mind the reasons for the concerns. Foremost is the perplexity as to how the biblical Scriptures can combine both narrative and prophetic instruction. The Qur'an is not narrative; it refers to historical events as parables, but historical narratives are not there. Muslims believe all true scripture has been sent down to earth from a "guarded tablet" in heaven. Scripture that contains historical narrative does not fit the Muslim paradigm. Other areas of perplexity are the many translations of the Bible, as well as the contradictions between the Bible and the Qur'an.

Noteworthy is the denial of the crucifixion of Jesus in the Qur'an, whereas a significant part of all four Gospels is about the crucifixion and resurrection.

The question of the trustworthiness of the Bible is fundamentally theological. Muslims believe Muhammad is just a tube through whom the Qur'an gushes. There is no human instrumentality except to be the conduit of the revelation. In the Bible, God himself comes down to meet us and to save us. The Bible is the account of salvation history, wherein human instrumentality is a lively reality. So a Muslim assertion that "the Bible has been altered" is really grounded in a fundamental divergence in our respective understandings of the essence of revelation.

Nevertheless, I believe it is helpful to respond constructively to Muslim concerns about the trustworthiness of the biblical Scriptures. I have observed in chapter 5 that nowhere does the Qur'an explicitly assert that Christians or Jews have altered the written texts. There are assertions in the Qur'an that people maliciously misquote or misinterpret the Bible. Two references are sometimes used; one warns Christians not to misquote the Bible and another warns against writing false scripture.[1] There are dire warnings of judgment for these deceivers. We accept those warnings and observe that these verses do not charge that the Bible itself has been altered.

It is helpful to observe the role of the Dead Sea Scrolls in proving that the Old Testament texts in our possession are a true transmission of the earliest Old Testament manuscripts. It is also helpful to mention that there are at least five thousand ancient manuscripts of the New Testament. From a study of the manuscripts, our scholars tell us the Bible is a true transmission of the original texts.[2]

However, the challenge persists! We cannot avoid the reality that there is a widespread assumption by Muslims that Christians and Jews have tampered with the original biblical texts that God entrusted to the People of the Book.

---

1. Qur'an: *Ali Imran* (The Family of Imran): surah 3:78; Qur'an: *Baqara* (The Heifer): surah 2:79.
2. David W. Shenk, *The Holy Book of God: An Introduction* (Achimota, Ghana: African Christian Press, 1981), 59–60.

In one of my mosque visits, the imam threw up his hands and declared, "There are too many references in the Qur'an that the Bible is corrupted to even mention!"

"Please," I implored, "give us one such reference." He could think of none.

In a mosque recently, the imam was belaboring the tragedy of Christians tampering with the texts of scripture. I turned to him and said, "Please listen for a moment to the wisdom of a man with gray hair. We all know God himself protects the scriptures. Both the Qur'an and the Bible say that. So let's drop this conversation about corruption of scripture and talk about what our scriptures teach." He agreed. We had a remarkable evening talking about the meaning of the incarnation and the cross in the Christian faith.

What do you mean by Son of God?

That takes us to the next question: what is the meaning of the incarnation? We must begin with a forthright disclaimer and affirmation. First, the Qur'an warns we should not believe God had a spouse who bore him a son. We agree with that warning. We do not believe God had a spouse who bore him a son.[3]

So what does it mean when the church confesses Jesus the Messiah is the Son of God? We should take note, for this name was given to Jesus by God. When the angel Gabriel announced the coming birth of the Messiah to the virgin Mary, the angel said he would be called the Son of God. (Note that the Qur'an also asserts Gabriel came to the virgin Mary to inform her that she was chosen to bear Jesus.) And twice in his ministry God spoke from heaven, saying Jesus is his beloved Son.[4]

I usually share two meanings of Jesus as the Son of God. First, he is the Word; second, he had a perfect relationship of oneness and fellowship with God.

The Qur'an refers to Jesus as the Word (*kalimatullah*). The Qur'an clarifies that this means Jesus is miraculously created by the word of God, just as God spoke and Adam was created.[5] So

---

3. Qur'an: *Nisaa* (Women): surah 4:171.
4. Bible: Luke 1:32; Matthew 3:17; Luke 9:35.
5. Qur'an: *Nisaa* (Women): surah 4:171.

when the Qur'an refers to the Messiah as the Word, it does not mean incarnation. It means God created Jesus in the womb of the virgin.

Nevertheless, we invite our Muslim friends to consider the biblical meaning of Jesus as the Word in the gospel. The gospel declares, "In the beginning was the Word, and the Word was with God, and the Word was God. He was with God in the beginning. Through him all things were made. . . . The Word became flesh and made his dwelling among us. We have seen his glory, the glory of the one and only Son, who came from the Father, full of grace and truth."[6] This means Jesus is truly the Word through whom God created and sustains the universe. Word has become human and we have seen that he is the "one and only Son who came from the Father."

It is impossible to separate God from his Word, who is the full expression of God. So God is one, for God and his Word are one. God cannot tell a lie. When we meet his Word, we are meeting the true and full revelation of God.

Yet there remains a huge perplexity. Muslims ask, "Where is the book, called the Gospel, Jesus brought from heaven? Alas! It must be Jesus took it back to heaven when he ascended."

When we open the New Testament, we discover four books called the Gospels: Matthew, Mark, Luke, John. There is no book called "The Gospel." Muslims are perplexed.

Christians must explain. Jesus never brought a book from heaven, for he *is* the book from heaven. Jesus the Messiah did not bring the gospel; he *is* the gospel. God sent Jesus, the living Word, from heaven into the world.

The four Gospel accounts were written by witnesses or associates of witnesses of Jesus the Messiah, who is the Gospel. God planned for there to be four written accounts of the life and teachings of Jesus so that we would know the truth of who he is. In a court, one witness is not enough; four witnesses establish the matter. The writing of the four Gospel accounts was inspired by the Holy Spirit of God. These four witnesses provide us with trustworthy accounts concerning Jesus the Messiah.

---

6. Bible: John 1:1-3, 14.

The second meaning of Son of God is that Jesus the Messiah had perfect love and fellowship with God. Jesus said, "I and the Father are one." He added, "When you have seen me, you have seen the Father."[7] Amazingly, when we believe in Jesus the Messiah, the Spirit of God brings us into loving communion with God, so we can also refer to God as our loving heavenly Father. Jesus has perfect communion with God. We also are invited to experience dimensions of the love of God that Jesus knew in perfection. That is why Christians address God as loving heavenly Father.

So Jesus as Son of God means he is the incarnation of the eternal Word of God, and it means Jesus has perfect fellowship and union with God.

Why do you refer to God as Trinity?

The third question Muslims often ask is the meaning of the Trinity. The answer to that question further explains the nature of Jesus as the Son of God. Recall that in Nairobi we lived on the same street as the mosque. One Friday after prayers, a young man came hurrying up to our house from the mosque, exclaiming, "It must stop! It must stop!"

I met him at our door and asked, "What must stop?"

"Your teaching about three gods must stop."

"Please explain. What do you mean? No one here is teaching there are three gods."

He exploded, "The Trinity! You must stop teaching about the Trinity."

I exclaimed, "Oh, the Trinity! Trinity is not about three gods. Actually, *Trinity* means that you and I should love each other. Let me explain. God is one and God is love. That means God is united in loving communion. Through the ministry of Jesus the Messiah, God has reached out to us sinners to reveal his love among us. In the resurrection power of the risen Messiah, God has sent the Holy Spirit to live among us and in us, so as to empower us to love one another as God loves. God does not sit with folded hands just keeping his love to himself. Oh, no! In Jesus, God comes down to save us and empower us to love as God

---

7. Bible: John 10:30; 14:9.

loves. That is what Trinity means: this name for God is our inadequate way of putting into language the reality that God is love."

The young man exclaimed in astonishment, "If that is what Trinity means, it is wonderful!" After that, whenever we met on the street, he would call me "Dear David."

The Qur'an has several references to the Holy Spirit.[8] Many Muslims assume these references to the Holy Spirit are about the angel Gabriel. However, credible Muslim scholarship persists in saying Muslims should recognize that the Qur'an does refer to the Holy Spirit or the Spirit of God.[9] It is helpful to recognize that God and his Spirit are one, and likewise, God and the Word are one. One way of expressing the Trinity is: God the Creator (Father), God the Spirit, and God the Word. Creator, Spirit, and Word are one.

How could the Messiah be crucified?

The question about the cross is related to the reality that God is love, a reality we try to express by the inadequate language of *Trinity*. The cross is the revelation of how great is the love of God. That is exactly the Muslim question about the crucifixion, because in Islam, God never comes down to rescue us. He never suffers for us or because of us. He is never affected by us. God is merciful and sends his will down, but God himself never reaches down to save us.

I often share with Muslims that the love of God revealed in the cross is so astonishing because no religion or philosophy has ever imagined God could love so greatly. For this reason, it is only the Holy Spirit who can open our eyes to the amazing love of God revealed in Jesus crucified and risen. We bear witness that those open arms of Jesus on the cross are the open arms of God in Christ, welcoming us to receive his forgiveness and reconciliation. He welcomes all to come.

Tremendous sacrifice

One evening a congregation in a Philadelphia mosque met for two hours of extra prayers. This was part of their Ramadan

8. Qur'an: *Baqara* (The Heifer): surah 2:87.
9. Abdullah Yusuf Ali, *The Holy Qur'an: Text, Translation, and Commentary* (Beirut Lebanon: Dar al Arabia, 1968), 1605–5677.

commitment. Late that evening when they concluded their prayers, the imam explained to those of us present that there is a balance scales. These extra prayers will go on the good side of the scales in preparation for the final judgment. But no one knows if one has said enough prayers.

I responded that we have observed that every year at the feast of sacrifice, Muslims offer thousands of rams around the world. They remember that God rescued a son of Abraham from death by providing a "momentous" substitutionary sacrifice, according to the Qur'an.[10] That account of God providing the sacrifice for a son of Abraham is in both the Torah and the Qur'an. We believe that sacrifice is a sign pointing to Jesus the Messiah, the Lamb of God who has taken our place. This is why Christians around the world bear witness that they are forgiven.

The imam objected. He pointed out that in a court, no one can take the place of the accused. "That is true," I observed. "But there is one exception. If the judge himself enters the courtroom and declares to the accused, 'I will take your place,' then the accused is free. In the Messiah, the righteous judge has entered the courtroom and taken our place."

The congregation sat in reverent silence. Then the imam observed, "This is too deep."

Surprising good news

About fifty Muslims and Christians were sitting in a circle on the carpeted floor of the Upper Darby Mosque in the Philadelphia suburbs. In a two-hour presentation, the imam described the six pillars of belief and six pillars of duty in Islam. He wrapped up the evening by saying, "You can forget everything I have said tonight. But there is one exception. Never forget that there is nothing surprising in Islam. It is the religion of the natural man. All of us are born naturally Muslim. Even without revelation, philosophy would open our eyes to the truth of Islam."

I responded, "That might be true of Islam, but that is not the gospel. The gospel is so surprising that we cannot believe it without the Holy Spirit opening our eyes to the amazement of

---

10. Qur'an: *Ya Sin*. surah 36:107; Bible: Genesis 22:9-14.

God's great love. The gospel is the good news that God has come to us in a baby in a manger, in a refugee in Egypt, in a carpenter in Nazareth, in a wandering preacher who often slept outside in the wilderness, in a man who washed the feet of the one who planned to betray him, in a man who when he was crucified cried out, 'Father forgive them!'"

The imam responded, "It is impossible for God to love that much!"

"Do not put God in a box and say he cannot love like Jesus loved," I urged. "Let God surprise you!"

How much does God love?

Each of these questions that Muslims bring to the table when meeting with Christians are in various ways about one central question: how much does God love? Our words are inadequate to describe the mystery and reality of God's love. There is much mystery in life. My fifty-five years of marriage to Grace are a mystery. I cannot explain the mystery of my marriage. Yet it is real and wonderful. The trinity of God is likewise a mystery. We believe in God as Trinity because we experience God as Father, Son, and Holy Spirit. Trinity is our inadequate effort to express in words the wonder of it all: that while we were yet sinners, Christ died for us that we may be reconciled to God![11]

Questions for discussion

1. Ponder the four questions Muslims usually bring to the table when meeting Christians. To what extent is there a unifying theme in the questions?

2. Why do Muslims so often ask the question: has the Bible been changed? Explain reasons why many Muslims are perplexed by the Bible as a scripture that includes historical narrative. How might a Christian explain why so much of the Bible is historical narrative?

3. Imagine you are having a strawberry sundae with a Muslim high school friend, and your friend asks, "Do you believe that Jesus is the Son of God?" What will she likely

---

11. Bible: Romans 5:8.

think you mean if you say, "Yes, I believe Jesus is the Son of God"? How might you explain Jesus as Son of God in a way your friend can understand?

4. Elaborate on this statement: God as Trinity means God is Love.

CHAPTER 8
Confront the Distortions

Grace and I were in a restaurant in an Asian country when friends ushered to our table another American couple. Our friends introduced me as an expert on Islam. "Oh, how delightful to meet you!" the American couple exclaimed. "We want to learn all we can from you about Muslims. Of course, we both know it is difficult to describe Muslims, because the Muslim holy book teaches Muslims to be liars. So when a Muslim says he has become a Christian, we can all know he is still a Muslim because his lies actually communicate the opposite of what is true."

On another occasion I was in a mosque on a Friday just on the eve of the Christmas holidays. In the sermon the imam confidently explained to the congregation that Christians get drunk on Christmas. So a proof of the truth of Islam is that Muslims do not get drunk, he said; they would never think of desecrating a Muslim festival by drinking.

Neither statement is true. Some Muslims do tell lies; some Christians do get drunk at Christmas. But this is not normal. Most Christians do not get drunk on Christmas, and most Muslims are not liars.

Muslims and Christians often participate in distortions of one another. Both would do well to be people of truth and avoid distortions or exaggerated overstatement.

Speak truthfully and kindly
When I am talking to a Christian audience, I imagine Badru Kateregga standing with me, listening to all I say. He is the Muslim

friend who wrote *A Muslim and a Christian in Dialogue* with me. That helps to keep me kind and truthful. If I know I am saying something about Islam that he would disagree with, I acknowledge publicly that what I am saying about Islam would not be supported by Muslims. My goal is to communicate the essence of Islam in ways that, if Muslims were listening, they would agree. I am committed to accurately describing their faith and truthfully representing disagreements. I also plead with Muslims to exercise the same commitment. Muslims and Christians should be careful to portray each other in ways that are truthful, kind, and trust building. We need to portray the beliefs and practices of Islam and the gospel in truthful ways.

Addressing Muslim distortions about the Holy Spirit
In the spirit of building relations committed to truth, I will comment on four distortions that need to be addressed: two Muslim distortions and two Christian distortions. First I will address a Muslim distortion and then a Christian distortion.

Muslims often comment that Jesus prophesied the coming of Muhammad. This conviction arises from the Qur'an stating that Jesus anticipated a final prophet. Muslims believe Muhammad is that prophet.[1] So Muslims search the New Testament to find where Jesus proclaimed that a final prophet would come. Muslim scholars say they have found the prophecy in John 14 and 16, where Jesus prophesied the coming of the Counselor.[2] The original Greek word is *paracleitos,* meaning "counselor." Muslim scholars sometimes state that they have discovered the original word is *periplutos,* meaning "the one worthy of praise." Ahmed, or Muhammad, also means "the one worthy of praise." These scholars explain that although the original word was *periplutos,* Christians removed *periplutos* and inserted a corruption of the text—namely, *paracleitos,* "the counselor."

Christians often experience this "scholarly" denial of Jesus' promise of the coming of the Holy Spirit. I was in a mosque when the imam began to weep as he explained to us that Christians had changed the text and inserted "the Holy Spirit" instead of the original "Muhammad." The imam demonstrated anguished grief

---

1. Qur'an: *Saf* (Battle Array): surah 61:6.
2. Bible: John 14:16-17; 16:7-11.

that Christians would do such a thing! How should Christians respond? We decided to address this distortion of the truth. This is how we responded in the mosque that evening:

> There are at least five thousand ancient manuscripts of the New Testament. All of these manuscripts, with no exception, assert that Jesus promised the Counselor would come and that the Counselor is the Holy Spirit. So we choose to stand upon the testimony of the Scriptures God has entrusted to us. And we encourage our Muslim friends likewise to respect the trustworthiness of the biblical account concerning the Holy Spirit.

We went on to explain that it is through the Holy Spirit we can know the truth. The Holy Spirit is one with God. So it is not wise to say the Holy Spirit is a man! The Holy Spirit is not a human being. He is the presence of God with us, through whom we can know the truth and be empowered to live the truth. So we implored this congregation of Muslims to desist from saying that the prophecy of the coming of the Holy Spirit is really a prophecy about a man, namely Muhammad. In fact, we read in one of the John 14 passages, "But the Advocate [Counselor], the Holy Spirit, whom the Father will send in my name, will teach you all things and will remind you of everything I have said to you."[3] We explained that it is through the Holy Spirit God convicts us of the truth. We need to avoid offending or disregarding the Holy Spirit.

Addressing Christian distortions about Allah

Another prevalent distortion comes to us from Christians. This distortion is the idea that Allah is not the God Christians worship. Some Christians go so far as to use terms related to Allah that I choose not to state in a published book. It is instructive to know that across the Middle East the Arab Christians all refer to God as Allah. In fact, it might be that Muhammad got the name *Allah* from the Christians. Some Christian inscriptions from pre-Islamic Arabia use Allah as the name for God.[4]

---

3. Bible: John 14:26.
4. Rick Brown, "Who Was Allah before Islam? Evidence the Term 'Allah' Originated with Jewish and Christian Arabs," in *Toward Respectful Understanding and Witness among Muslims,* Evelyne A. Reisacher, ed., (Pasadena, CA: William Carey Library, 2012), 164–78.

Where did these Christians and Muslims get the name Allah? Most likely this is a legacy from Abraham, who referred to God almighty as *Eloha*.[5] Allah is the Arabic way of saying *Eloha*. Muhammad taught that he had a mission to establish worship of the one true God, the God of Abraham, throughout Arabia and in regions beyond Arabia. His message was that there is only one God almighty, creator of the heavens and the earth. His name is *Eloha* (Allah).

However, we need to recognize that in the Christian missionary movement around the world, the church has used many names for God, not just the Arabic *Allah*. When Christian missionaries go around the world testifying about God, with rare exception, they seek for a local name for God. They resist bringing a new name. If possible, Bible translators use the local name for the Creator. Islam is different.

Muslims always bring their Arabic name for God, Allah. But with rare exception, the church uses a local name for God. The reason that the church looks for a local name for God is the conviction God has a witness within every culture and religion.

For example, when my parents went to the Zanaki people of Tanzania as Christian missionaries, they asked the Zanaki people whether they knew about God. They assured my parents they were aware of God. They called the Creator *Murungu*. They believed that *Murungu* had gone away and would never return again. My parents, therefore, used *Murungu* when they translated the gospel of Matthew into the Zanaki language. They preached that in Jesus, there is a full revelation of *Murungu*. They never said the God of the Bible is a different god from *Murungu*. Rather, they preached that in Jesus the Messiah, *Murungu* has come near and lives among us.

A helpful biblical explanation of what I am saying is the account of God meeting Moses at the burning bush.[6] And later we read, "God said to Moses, 'I am the Lord. I appeared to Abraham, to Isaac and to Jacob as God Almighty, but by my name the Lord I did not make myself fully known to them.'"[7] God is proclaiming he is God almighty (Allah or *Eloha*). All faithful Jews, Christians,

5. Ibid., 147–63.
6. Bible: Exodus 3.
7. Bible: Exodus 6:2-3.

and Muslims believe in God almighty, the creator of the heavens and the earth.

But with Moses, God revealed himself not only as God our almighty Creator (Allah) but as the God who comes down to save us. He comes down to meet us and to reveal himself to us. This is God as the Good Shepherd, who comes down to seek his lost sheep. This is God as *Yahweh* (the Lord), who reveals that his essence is love.[8]

A God who reveals his essence and who comes down to save us is hard for Muslims to fathom. Recently I was in a major dialogue with university students in Bandung, Indonesia. My Muslim dialogue companions asserted that in Islam, God sends his perfect will down but never comes down to save us. There was no room in their thinking for the suffering love of God. For that reason, my dialogue companions denied the crucifixion of Jesus. In the biblical Scriptures we meet God in the Messiah, coming down to suffer with us and because of us. My dialogue companions found that hard to comprehend. The mostly Muslim university students were amazed at the gospel's revelation that God loves so greatly he offers forgiveness and reconciliation for those who put Jesus on the cross.

Christians believe our understandings of God are never as complete as when we meet God as revealed in the Bible and especially as revealed in the Messiah. For example, Jesus the Messiah reveals that we are invited to know and address God as our loving heavenly Father. That is a prayer Muslims do not pray. So to say Christians and Muslims worship the same God is true. However, we cannot say the perceptions or experience of God are the same as God revealed in Jesus the Messiah. The great surprise of the gospel is that in Jesus, God, our loving heavenly Father, has come down to save us and to meet us and reveal himself to us.

In the gospel we learn Jesus is the Savior from sin. He is also called *Emmanuel*, which means "God with us." He is called Messiah, which means he is the one anointed by God to bring about God's righteous kingdom on earth. He is *Eloha* or Allah, the almighty creator God. All these names are glimpses into the person and mission of Jesus.

---

8. Bible: 1 John 4:16.

Of course, we all recognize that God cannot be captured in a name. Neither Allah nor *Eloha* nor Yahweh nor *Murungu* can communicate the essence of who God is. God is beyond naming. That is why God announced to Moses that his name is "I AM!"[9] Although God is beyond naming, nevertheless God reveals himself in the Bible. This is why Christians confess God as our loving heavenly Father. This reality goes beyond any name. It is in the revelation of God in Jesus that we know God as our Father.

Addressing Muslim distortions of scripture

Two other distortions demand comment. These distortions come about in the way Muslims and Christians handle the scriptures. First, I will describe a Muslim distortion.

Muslims have a high view of scripture, and some are concerned about the differences between the Bible and the Qur'an. That was the reason a dear Muslim friend gave me a book neatly wrapped in gift paper. We were having lunch together when he presented this special gift. I was disturbed when I opened the wrapping to find the *Gospel of Barnabas*. This book is about the size of the New Testament. It is a description of the life and teachings of Jesus, mostly following the Muslim script as presented in the Qur'an. For example, in this gospel Jesus is not crucified. Some apocryphal material is included, such as Jesus making birds of clay and then bringing them to life.

The book seems to have appeared in the fourteenth century. There are absolutely no ancient texts of this "gospel." One theory by credible Christian scholars conjectures that the author was a disillusioned Catholic priest who wrote the document hoping to lead Christians away from the New Testament and into the embrace of Islam.[10] In my judgment, this gospel is what the Qur'an describes as false scripture.[11]

As my friend handed me the book he said, "This book will reveal to you the true gospel of Jesus."

---

9. Bible: Exodus 3:14.
10. Selim Abdul-Ahad and W. H. T. Gairdner, *The Gospel of Barnabas: An Essay and Inquiry* (Hyderabad: Henry Martyn Institute of Islamic Studies, 1975). Oddbjørn Leirvik, "History as a Literary Weapon: The Gospel of Barnabas in Muslim-Christian Polemics" in *Studia Theologica* 56, no. 1 (2002): 4–26.
11. Qur'an: *Baqara* (The Heifer): surah 2:79.

I thanked him for the gift, for I knew he was giving me this book out of concern that I would know the whole truth of God. With the book in my hand, I asked him, "What does the Qur'an say about writing and circulating false scripture?"

My friend forcefully exclaimed, "God will damn all such people!"

I asked, "Then why have you given me this book? If you investigate, I believe you will discover this is false scripture, written probably about seven hundred years ago. There are no ancient manuscripts of this book. It is a distortion of the gospel as written in the New Testament Scriptures."

He exclaimed, "Forgive me; I did not know."

This distortion is serious. This book is distributed around the world. It needs to be addressed whenever this "gospel" is circulated. We plead with people not to circulate false scriptures like the *Gospel of Barnabas*.

Addressing Christian distortions of the Qur'an

The other serious distortion comes to us from Christians who claim to have understood the meaning and message of the Qur'an even though they know no Arabic. We need to remember that the Qur'an is revealed in Arabic. To understand the true meaning of the Qur'an, one needs to know Arabic! Muslim communities have *ulama* (theologians), who are recognized as wise men with insight based on a thorough knowledge of the Qur'an. These wise men also study the *hadith* ("the Traditions") that describe the way Muhammad applied Qur'anic principles in his personal conduct. However, even the *ulama* do not make judgments about the meaning of the Qur'an based on individual insight. All insight is gleaned through the process of group study and consensus. For this reason I lean on Muslim writers and imams for my understanding of Islam and interpretation of the Qur'an.

I grieve, as do Muslims, when Christians take an English interpretation of the Qur'an and determine that they have come to understand the meaning of this scripture. To understand the meaning, there is only one acceptable and wise way; that is to ask the Muslim *ulama* to explain the Qur'an to those of us who are not Muslim. This is urgent. It is not wise or appropriate to claim we have come to understand the Qur'an unless we have submitted to the rugged disciplines of study and consensus that Muslims believe are necessary to understand the Qur'an's message.

We also need to recognize that there is much variation in the understandings and application of the Qur'an. There is immense diversity within the global Muslim movement concerning the interpretation of the Qur'an. Some Muslim feminists embrace a modernist secularist commitment and might perform the required prayers once a year. In contrast, there are Arabian Wahhabists, who insist a true Qur'anic interpretation means a woman may not drive a car. More than one billion Muslims are scattered around the world; they are a movement of incredible diversity. Yet I suppose all Muslims would agree that the Qur'an is God's final revelation of his will and Muhammad is the perfect example of what it means to submit to the will of God.

My caution is that we do not presume a reading of the Qur'an means we have understood it. Nevertheless, the caution does not mean those who do not know Arabic should exclude themselves from reading or studying interpretations of the Qur'an in their own languages. But when we do so, we need to approach the study with humility and an awareness of our limitations.

Quite frequently in my conversations with Muslims, I mention an English interpretation of a verse or portion in the Qur'an and ask them to explain the meaning of that selection. Then I ask if I may share from the Scriptures used in the life of the church. An example is the virgin birth of Jesus the Messiah. We might ask our Muslim friends to comment on the significance of the virgin birth of Jesus. Then we may offer as believers in Jesus what the *Injil* (gospel) reveals about the virgin birth of the Messiah.

Explore the message of the scriptures

I do not know Arabic, but I keep English interpretations of the Qur'an on my desk and refer to them often. The indexes in the back of my Qur'an are helpful in identifying themes I want to study. For study purposes I rely on Abdullah Yusuf Ali, because he has useful notes and commentary. However, I get my most reliable information from Muslim friends who know the Qur'an well.

Christians do not need to know the biblical languages of Greek or Hebrew before they begin a study of the Bible. For many years I have practiced daily reading of the Bible in my mother tongue, English. These Scriptures form me. My commitment to the Bible also immensely enhances my credibility with Muslims. Recall that the Qur'an refers to those who believe the biblical Scriptures as "People of the Book." It is an honor to be known as a person of the Book.

Cultivate goodwill

I have described several examples of distortions. Christians should address distortions, whether from the Muslim or the Christian communities. Muslims, likewise, have responsibility to address distortions that Muslims or Christians might carry. Distortions can be enormously destructive. Let us learn the art of listening to one another in ways that open our eyes to the distortions to which we might have become party. We need to speak the truth and use our tongues in ways that build trust. We can use our tongues to fan the flames of discord or to enhance good relations.

The apostle Peter advises, "Whoever would love life and see good days must keep their tongue from evil and their lips from deceitful speech."[12] We need to be truth tellers who avoid distortions!

Questions for discussion

1. Consider other distortions Muslims or Christians should address.
2. Respond to this statement: the Christian God is not the God whom Muslims worship.
3. Ponder ways you appreciate Muslims. How does it make you feel when people speak unkindly about the church or when they speak unkindly about the Muslim community?
4. How should a Christian respond when a Muslim says that Jesus prophesied the coming of Muhammad?
5. Consider practical ways a Christian could become acquainted with the message of the Qur'an. How might a Muslim become acquainted with the message of the Bible?

12. Bible: 1 Peter 3:10.

CHAPTER 9

Consider the Choice: The *Hijrah*. The Cross.

Two different narratives form the ways Islam and the gospel commit to establishing the will of God on earth. Both the *umma* and the church are movements committed to bringing every area of life under the authority of God. However, the way to bring about this reality takes Muslims and disciples of Jesus in opposite directions.

In 2001, just after the attack on the World Trade Center in New York City, I asked Mark Oxbrow, a director of the Church Missionary Society in the United Kingdom, "What do you preach about in England in times like these?"

His immediate response was, "Three journeys: Jesus to Jerusalem, Muhammad to Medina, Constantine to Rome. We must each decide which of these three journeys we will follow."

Since that conversation I have preached about these three different journeys around the world.[1]

Muhammad: from Mecca to Medina

First we reflect on the journey Muhammad chose. For twelve years Muhammad preached in Mecca. He claimed the angel

---

1. This chapter is an adaptation and development of the theme that I have written about in various versions. The most comprehensive description I have written of these different journeys is "Three Journeys—Jesus, Constantine, Muhammad," in *Anabaptists Meeting Muslims: A Calling for Presence in the Way of Christ,* James R. Krabill, David W. Shenk, Linford Stutzman, eds. (Scottdale, PA: Herald Press, 2005), 25–47. That essay is adapted here with permission.

Gabriel appeared to him from time to time, revealing the Qur'an segment by segment. The first message was brief:

> Read: in the name of thy Lord who createth, createth man
> from a clot.
> Read: and thy Lord is the Most bounteous, who teacheth
> by the pen, teacheth man which he knew not.[2]

As the revelations came, Muhammad proclaimed these messages faithfully. He insisted only that Allah is God and people should abandon the worship of polytheistic divinities. Yet he was not successful in establishing the house of Islam. There were 360 divinities in the grand temple (*Ka'bah*) in the center of Meccan polytheism. The Meccan Muslims were discouraged by their lack of success and the serious threats against their lives. Then messengers came to Mecca from Medina, about 275 miles north of Mecca. They invited Muhammad to come to Medina as their prophet, political leader, and military commander. This seemed to the Muslims to be providential, for such a move would provide Muhammad with the political mechanisms and the spiritual authority to establish the house of Islam.

Muhammad accepted the invitation. He and his disciples secretly commenced the three-week journey to Medina. This secret migration from Mecca to Medina is the *hijrah*, and it is the beginning of the Muslim era. Muslims do not begin their era with the birth of Muhammad in AD 570, or with the first revelation through Gabriel in AD 610. Rather, the era begins with the migration to Medina.

Muslims explain to me that the *hijrah* is actually the most significant event in the history of the world, because for the first time a prophet of God acquired political and military power sufficient to establish a region obedient to the will of God. This region had political systems that could potentially extend to include the whole world. Muslims point out that Moses only managed to put a political system in place that included Israel. Jesus did not even try to establish a political system.

---

2. Qur'an: *Iqraa* (Proclaim): surah 96:1-5.

When Muhammad and his group of followers arrived in Medina, the town welcomed them enthusiastically. Quickly Muhammad acquired political authority, and he used that power effectively to establish the house of Islam. During the next eight years there were numerous battles between the Meccans and the Muslims. In one battle, the Muslims were defeated. The Qur'an explains that the faithful Muslim community will never be defeated; hence, the defeat was because the soldiers had not adequately followed the command of Muhammad. Furthermore, the army was consoled by a Qur'anic revelation informing the community that those who died in battle for the *umma* would go immediately to paradise.[3]

It is in this context that Muslims developed the conviction that Jesus the Messiah was never crucified. In Mecca, when Muhammad had no political and military power, the Muslims were blocked in their efforts to establish a robust community.[4] However, after the *hijrah,* when he acquired political and military power, he was empowered to establish the *umma.* As we can see, a theology that says political and military power were necessary for Muhammad to succeed is quite different from a theology proclaiming that the foolishness of the cross is the power of God![5]

For the next eight years, intermittent battles with the Meccan polytheists continued on the periphery. Over time, these regions in conflict with the Muslims were referred to as the regions of war (*dar al harb*). Kenneth Cragg comments, *"Dar al Islam* and *Dar al Harb* is a fundamental distinction running through all humanity; the household of submission to God and the household of non-Islam still to be brought into such submission."[6]

The Qur'an gives specific instructions on dealing with aggressors who are attacking the *umma.* "Fight in the way of Allah against those who fight against you, . . . And fight them until persecution is no more, and religion is for Allah. But if they desist, then let there be no hostility except against wrongdoers."[7] This

---

3. Qur'an: *Anfal* (The Spoils of War): surah 8:5-19; *Ali Imran* (The Family of Imran): surah 3:169-79.

4. Tamim Ansary, *Destiny Disrupted: A History of the World through Muslim Eyes* (New York: PublicAffairs, 2009).

5. Bible: 1 Corinthians 1:18-25.

6. Kenneth Cragg, *The Call of the Minaret* (Maryknoll, NY: Orbis Books, 1985), 189.

7. Qur'an: *Baqara (*The Heifer): surah 2:190-93.

surah was proclaimed at a time when the Muslim *umma* was severely threatened by enemies; another *surah*, however, exalts that reconciliation is best![8]

In spite of the battles on the periphery, Muhammad set about the business of establishing the *umma* in Medina. He led in the development of a constitution that included the rights of non-Muslims within the house of Islam. It was a tremendous disappointment for the Muslims when they came to the conclusion that the Jewish community did not support the development of the house of Islam. Subsequently, Jews were banished from Medina and its environs. The several hundred Jews suspected of planning the destruction of the *dar al Islam* were dealt with just as governments deal with those suspected of treason.[9]

Finally, the Meccans asked for peace. A treaty was signed. Muhammad now entered the city in triumph. He was accompanied by ten thousand soldiers; many were mounted cavalry. Muhammad forgave all who had been fighting against him, except for several detractors. He and his army entered the *Ka'bah* and smashed all the gods within the temple. The peace accord, agreed upon before he and his army entered the *Ka'bah*, assured a peaceful occupation. The Qur'an exalts, "Truth has (now) Arrived and Falsehood perished: For Falsehood is (by its nature) Bound to perish."[10]

By the time of Muhammad's death in 632, the *dar al Islam* had extended political control over Arabia; within a century, Islamic rule extended from the Indus River, across North Africa and the Iberian Peninsula, to the Pyrenees Mountains of Spain.

Jesus: from Galilee to Jerusalem

Six hundred years earlier, Jesus the Messiah had faced a similar choice to that of Muhammad, but he chose to go in the opposite direction. For nearly three years Jesus had been preaching the gospel of the kingdom throughout Israel. He was becoming quite popular in his home region of Galilee. His popularity grew

---

8. Qur'an: *Nisaa* (Women): surah 4:128.
9. Alfred Guillaume, *The Life of Muhammad*, 231–33.
10. Qur'an: *Bani Israil* (The People of Israel): surah 17:81.

greatly when he miraculously fed five thousand men plus women and children by breaking and multiplying five loaves of bread and two fish. (Probably twenty thousand were miraculously fed that day.) With that miracle, all of Galilee was getting on the bandwagon, believing he was most likely the Messiah foretold by the prophets. They believed the Messiah would deliver Israel from Roman governance and extend God's peaceable kingdom to the ends of the earth.

After the miracle of feeding some twenty thousand people, the fans of Jesus attempted to make him become their king by force. There was an underground army fighting the Romans in Galilee. They were called Zealots, and were attempting to overpower their Roman rulers who worshiped many gods. The Zealots wanted to establish the rule of God on earth, free from oppression by polytheists. With the miraculous power he wielded, Jesus could feed the entire Zealot army and strike the Romans blind while leading Israel into victory over their enemies. It was a wonderful plan.

But Jesus rejected the plan. He left them immediately. That night he sent his disciples across the Sea of Galilee in a boat, while he spent the night in prayer. Shortly afterward, he told his disciples he was going to Jerusalem, where he would be crucified. Jesus said, "They will mock him, insult him and spit on him; they will flog him and kill him. On the third day he will rise again."[11] Peter objected strongly. The disciples could not comprehend that the Messiah would be crucified. Recall that this is the same objection to the crucifixion of Jesus that comes from Muslims; they also believe the Messiah cannot be crucified. Jesus rebuked Peter strongly, saying he did not understand the ways of God.

When Jesus arrived on the outskirts of Jerusalem, he mounted a colt. This was in fulfillment of a prophecy Zechariah proclaimed years earlier:

> Rejoice greatly, Daughter Zion!
> Shout, Daughter Jerusalem!
> See, your king comes to you,
> righteous and victorious,
> lowly and riding on a donkey,

---

11. Bible: Luke 18:32-33.

on a colt, the foal of a donkey.
I will take away the chariots from Ephraim
and the warhorses from Jerusalem,
and the battle bow will be broken.
He will proclaim peace to the nations.
His rule will extend from sea to sea
and from the River to the ends of the earth.[12]

Jesus was accompanied by an army of singing children.[13] As he neared the brow of the mount overlooking Jerusalem, he began to cry, for Jerusalem would not receive his peace. He then entered the temple and cleansed the temple of the merchants who had overtaken this place of worship. Rejoicing children accompanied him. Jesus then made it clear to the authorities that this temple would be no more. He prophesied a new temple. Every rock in the temple built of stone would be overthrown. This means that, for followers of Jesus, a temple in Jerusalem is not necessary. The true temple is not a rock or a building but the people of God, in whom God dwells through the Holy Spirit!

Events unfolded rapidly after Jesus' arrival in Jerusalem. He met for a last supper with the disciples and revealed that a disciple, Judas, would betray him to the authorities. Jesus rose from the table and washed the feet of his disciples, including Judas! Then, that evening in the Garden of Olives near the city wall, soldiers led by Judas came to arrest Jesus. Peter tried to protect Jesus by drawing a sword and cutting off the ear of the servant of the high priest. Jesus rebuked Peter; he healed the severed ear, and declared that the use of the sword is not the way of the kingdom of God he was establishing.

The next day Jesus was crucified between two thieves on a hill outside the walls of Jerusalem. As he died, Jesus cried out in forgiveness for those who had crucified him. In his cry of forgiveness, all who come to Jesus are likewise offered the grace of forgiveness. Outstretched arms are for embracing; they speak of invitation and forgiveness; they are an invitation to reconciliation.

God raised this Jesus, the Messiah, from the dead. After that,

---

12. Bible: Zechariah 9:9-10.
13. Bible: Luke 19:37-44; Matthew 21:1-17.

Jesus met the disciples in multiple appearances. In one of his appearances he proclaimed, "Peace be with you! As the Father has sent me, I am sending you. Receive the Holy Spirit."[14]

This is the mission of the church: to serve as Jesus the Messiah served, with the power of the Holy Spirit, in our broken world. The church is called to be a continuation of the kingdom of God that Jesus inaugurated. His kingdom is not established by weapons of war but is centered in the suffering, reconciling love of Jesus himself. In his crucifixion he has taken upon himself the sins of the world and offers forgiveness. This is the good news of the gospel the church around the world is called to proclaim.

Constantine: the march into Rome

Three centuries after the Messiah ascended into heaven, there was a most dramatic transformation of the meaning of the cross, which in time has significantly affected Christian-Muslim relations. Constantine was a Roman general who wanted to become emperor of the Roman Empire. He was ready to go into battle against his enemy, Maxentius, who also wanted to be emperor. Constantine claimed he saw a vision of the cross of Christ in the sky with the instructions, "Under this sign, conquer." That night Constantine ordered his troops to paint the sign of the cross on their shields. He went into battle under the sign of the cross and won the war. Constantine became emperor of the Western Roman Empire.

Up to that time, imperial authorities often persecuted Christians because they would not worship the gods of the empire, such as the genius of the emperor. Furthermore, before Constantine, Christians were often persecuted because of their refusal to participate in the military. For the first three hundred years of the Christian movement, believers generally did not serve in the military. They prayed for the governing authorities, but they did not bear arms.

Eventually the unthinkable happened. Christian soldiers under the sign of the cross went to war against Muslims! These wars, known as the Crusades, happened about a thousand years

---

14. Bible: John 20:21-22.

ago. But the memory of these horrible wars lives on in the hearts of multitudes of Muslims. This means that for many Muslims the cross is a sign of killing Muslims, not a sign of the redemptive love of God.

A Muslim theologian once rebuked me sharply for saying the cross is a revelation of the redemptive love of God for us. I had given a presentation in which I described the journey of Jesus from Galilee to Jerusalem, where he was crucified. I said, "At the cross, the sin and rebellion of the whole world was poured out upon the Messiah as he cried out in forgiveness."

The theologian stood up and said with deep anger, "I never knew the cross means forgiveness. I have always thought the cross means kill your enemy, and especially kill the Muslims."

I wept. At that time Kosovo was in flames. The Serbian militia was pummeling Muslim Kosovars who were fleeing their homes by the tens of thousands. The militia would enter Muslim villages, kill everyone, burn the villages, and plant crosses in the ashes. Those crosses in the ashes of destroyed Muslim villages were an announcement that Christian militia were responsible for the destruction. I knew the anger of the theologian was not only about wars fought a thousand years ago but also about current wars.

I responded, "What a horrible distortion of the cross of Christ that would lead Muslims to believe the essence of the cross is war against enemies and Muslims. May God forgive! May Muslims forgive!"

I thank God for Muslims I know who do view the cross as a revelation of love for one's enemies. Not all Muslims believe the violence of the Constantinian cross is a revelation of the suffering cross of Jesus.

After a three-hour break our consultation commenced again. The Muslim presenter said, "The confession and repentance we have heard for the sins of the church against us Muslims has opened my eyes to a Jesus I did not know about. I have been transformed. I do not know where this will take me, but I am forever grateful."

Which journey will we choose?

On a flight from Cairo to Istanbul, my seat companions were two men deeply engaged in the anti-Assad rebel movement in Syria. They introduced themselves, including their specific responsibilities in the movement. I responded by saying I was a believer in Jesus the Messiah and was committed to bear witness to his peace.

For the next hour, we three engaged in lively conversation about ultimate questions. The rebels insisted that the way of Jesus is utterly naive. The only realistic approach was more rockets from President Obama! I pleaded with them, saying the direction they were going guaranteed generations of hatred in the years to come. I urged them to consider the Jesus alternative. People around us were listening in on our conversation. I suppose they were hearing a discussion the likes of which they had never heard before. The issues of justice in a violent and unjust world were quite clear in that discussion—commitment to retribution or commitment to reconciliation. As far as my seat companions were concerned, retribution trumped all other alternatives.

That airplane conversation took me back some thirty years to an evening conversation with students in a tea shop in Somalia. The students asserted, "Peacemaking requires political and military power so that one can destroy the enemy."

I entreated, "Consider the way of Jesus, who invites us to forgive those who have done us wrong." I pointed out that if we go down the road of retribution, the cycles of violence will never stop.

They argued, "If we are honest, we need to say that the way of Jesus you are describing is not practical in our real world."

My challenge within that tea drinking circle was, "Investigate! What is the fruit of a commitment to retribution? Are you sure that the way of Jesus is impractical?"

We have looked at three journeys, all committed to the quest for the good. I believe the life-giving journey, the journey that speaks healing and hope to our modern world, is that of Jesus, whose open-wounded hands invite us to come to him. In Jesus there is forgiveness and reconciliation at the deepest levels of our lives.

Questions for discussion

1. Why has the Muslim movement generally turned away from believing that Jesus the Messiah was crucified?

2. Comment on this statement: Jesus' journey to Jerusalem and Muhammad's journey to Medina lead in opposite directions. What is the practical significance for peacemaking of these different journeys?

3. What is the difference between peacemaking that embraces the crucifixion of Jesus and peacemaking that denies the crucifixion of Jesus?

4. How is the mission of a Christ-centered church different from that of Muslims committed to Muhammad's approach in Medina? How is it different from a Constantinian approach to peacemaking?

5. Consider ways that Muslim peacemakers might draw upon Muhammad's experience in Mecca in looking for helpful approaches to peacemaking.

6. Account for the anger of the Muslim theologian at the seminar about the meaning of the cross. How would you respond?

CHAPTER 10
Seek Peace and Pursue It

In 1969 and the early 1970s, Marxist ideology began to extend its strangling tentacles throughout Somalia. A day came when all schools in Somalia were nationalized. Our schools became government schools; our headquarters and residences became government property. Our vehicles, including the mission's motor scooter, were taken. The officer who came to take the scooter did not know how to ride it, so I volunteered to take him to the office that was acquiring the scooter. He rode on the back, and I walked home after delivering the scooter. Surrendering the scooter meant much inconvenience, as did moving out of our properties into rental housing.

We cooperated. In contrast, most private Muslim schools resisted the government. Somalis were perplexed. They asked, "Why are you cooperating when other educational agencies are resisting?"

My response was, "We long to serve among the Somali people in the way of Jesus, who served without restraint."

We have often pondered whether our spirit of cooperation revealed more about the essence of the way of the Messiah than about the educational institutions we had developed. Those institutions were important. But the powerlessness of having everything taken, as we submitted to decisions of the governing authorities, spoke powerfully to the Somali people.

We learned new dimensions of what it meant to be guests. For example, one evening a decorated military officer suddenly appeared out of the darkness, calling for me to open our back door.

I invited him in for tea. I knew the officer; some years earlier I had taught him geography in one of our schools. I had heard he had gotten a degree in Moscow and was now back in Mogadishu, and I assumed he likely held a key role in the revolution.

The officer declined the tea and remained standing as he addressed me. "I have come tonight to ask you one question. Is the Marxist revolution a good thing for Somalia?"

As we so often did in such circumstances, I prayed for the Holy Spirit's guidance. In my soul I believed the revolution was reprehensible, especially the public executions of key leaders in Somali society. I also knew that what I said might determine whether we would be sent out of the country. Most other Westerners, such as those serving with the Peace Corps, had already left. At that time forty people were still serving with the Somalia Mennonite Mission (SMM).

I responded, "We are guests in your country. A guest should not comment on his hosts except to thank the host for his hospitality. So I have no comment on your question except to thank you and the Somali people for the hospitality we experience. If you want to know if the revolution is a good thing for the Somali people, ask your fellow Somalis. They will know the answer to your question. We want to serve in ways pleasing to God and a blessing to the Somali people. We are honored to live and serve among the Somali people, and we will continue to serve as long as we are welcomed."

He shook my hand and said, "I wish all Western people felt like you do about serving our people. You are to be thanked. Goodnight."

He was gone. I never saw him again. We continued to have a presence in Somalia for the next seven years and still serve the Somali people.

Choosing the way of Jesus

The journey of Jesus from Galilee to Jerusalem profoundly formed the early church.

Likewise, the decision of SMM to cooperate with the revolution's authorities was a decision to follow in the way of Jesus. He did not accept political power in Galilee and instead journeyed to

Jerusalem, where he met crucifixion. When the director of SMM was killed ten years earlier, this journey also formed the response of his widow, who had been wounded. She was in the hospital, struggling for her own life, when the assailant was brought to court. She sent a letter to the judge stating that she had forgiven the assailant and would press no charges. The court and the nation were astounded. Her offering of forgiveness touched the Somali nation deeply.

The foundation of all New Testament ethics is grounded in the reality that Jesus chose the way of the cross rather than the way of domineering self-interest. Some years after the crucifixion and resurrection of Jesus, Paul wrote to the church in Philippi, where two women were in conflict. Paul admonished the church, "Do nothing out of selfish ambition or vain conceit. Rather, in humility value others above yourselves, not looking to your own interests but each of you to the interests of the others. In your relationships with one another, have the same mindset as Christ Jesus."[1] Then he elaborated on Christ becoming a servant and giving his life in suffering on the cross. This theme—identifying with Jesus the Messiah in his spirit of servanthood and ministry of suffering—permeates all New Testament ethics.

The church is referred to as the body of Christ. What does that mean? It means the disciples of Jesus who are known as the church are called to continue the ministries of serving and suffering that Jesus modeled. This means that, in various ways, all disciples of Jesus take the journey of Jesus from Galilee to the cross. This commitment is exceedingly practical and powerfully transforming.

The meaning of the cross

Once, a team of Christian theologians was in a formal public dialogue with several Muslim scholars who counseled, "We Muslims believe Jesus was not crucified. So if you do not refer to the cross, that would open the door for true collaboration. Let's just consider the cross as an irrelevant difference."

I objected, saying, "If you remove the cross from the Christian faith, you take the soul out of the gospel." Then I said I would

---

1. Bible: Philippians 2:3-5.

illustrate that reality by telling about a recent event on a Sunday morning in a large refugee camp. I was to preach to a congregation of about 150 children and women; the men had mostly died in the conflict that was creating the refugee crisis.

This was my sermon: "In Jesus the Messiah, God has come down into your refugee camp and is participating in every way with your suffering. The Messiah was born in a cattle stall; your children have been born under thorn trees. When the Messiah was a child, his boyhood playmates were killed, just as the friends of your children have died. The Messiah was a refugee, just as you have become refugees. The Messiah traveled from place to place, sometimes probably using a stone as a pillow, just as you in your wanderings have done. The Messiah was beaten and killed, with his body hung on a tree, just as your husbands have been mutilated and hung on trees to die. In every way, God, in the Messiah, is participating in your suffering. But God raised the Messiah from the dead; he offers forgiveness for those who so abused him. Likewise, God through his Spirit empowers you to also arise from your terrible tragedy and move forward in hope. He invites and empowers you to forgive just as the Messiah forgives, so your souls will not be wounded by bitterness and anger."

After the preaching, those widows and their children went into the courtyard and for the next half hour they sang praises to Jesus and danced with joy. They sang in the presence of the church, which was the life-giving community of Jesus saving these women and their children from destruction. I asked the Muslim scholars, "Would there have been joyous singing that Sunday if I had preached that Jesus the Messiah escaped suffering, even though the widows needed to suffer?"

The identification of the Messiah with our suffering is a powerful dimension of the good news the church proclaims. As I understand Islam, God does not participate in our suffering. Although God is understood to be merciful, he does not come down to meet us and he is not affected by our situation. The songs of the widows, however, were their response to the Messiah who comes down to suffer with us and because of us. In his resurrection he triumphs over death and arises to new life. Likewise, through his Spirit, he enables the oppressed to arise and live triumphantly over the injustices that have trampled them. This is one central meaning of the cross: God participates in our suffering and empowers us to triumph over oppression.

There are other themes within the message of the cross. I cannot adequately expound on these various themes, which include forgiveness, reconciliation, redemption, atonement, the kingdom of God, and triumph over the powers. I comment on only two dimensions here: reconciliation and forgiveness.

Reconciled and forgiven

The Messiah forgave those who had betrayed and crucified him. The huge temptation for the refugee widows would be to let bitterness and anger destroy their souls. Wondrously, in the cross of Christ and the fullness of the Holy Spirit, those widows were experiencing release from resentful hatred. They were participating in the healing presence of the Messiah who turns revenge into a spirit of forgiveness. The songs and dances of praise to Jesus testified that these women, who had experienced unspeakable atrocities, were receiving the healing grace of the Messiah.

The cross is also God's way of bringing down barriers of hostility and building bridges of peacemaking. We live at a time in which the wrath of nations is pulling societies apart, often with vengeful repercussions. It is in this kind of world that these women are called to be peacemakers. This is the calling of God upon the church. Paul writes, "We are therefore Christ's ambassadors, as though God were making his appeal through us. We implore you on Christ's behalf: Be reconciled to God."[2]

Choosing hate

Forgiveness and reconciliation are miracles. They are not the "normal" way. Grace and I experienced that reality recently in conversations with a couple who had fled their homeland after the horrendous Srebrenica, Bosnia, genocide of 1995. Fifty of the man's cousins had died. We were appalled as we heard the stories of horror. They concluded by saying, "We want to die hating those who ruined our families and our lives."

---

2. Bible: 2 Corinthians 5:20.

We responded gently, "This is a heavy burden to carry—the burden of hate for the rest of your lives. Jesus offers release from the burden of bitterness which can destroy our souls."

They objected. "We do not want the Jesus way," they said decisively. "If it is ever possible, we will take revenge. We will never forgive."

We grieved as we parted that evening. We pondered what it means to walk through life with souls bound by such bitterness. We also recognized that we are privileged to have never experienced such horrendous atrocities. We have never experienced the struggle to forgive those who have committed such crimes.

Indonesian peacemakers

We thank God for the many we know around the world who are choosing another way. These are peace ambassadors who are engaged in building bridges amid abundant polarizations.

One example is Indonesia. For some years whenever I visited Indonesia I would hear of church burnings and sometimes of the death of a pastor. Solo, in Central Java, was an epicenter of the conflict between Christians and Muslims.[3] In that context, several Christian and Muslim leaders covenanted to work together for the peace of their city. One effort was mass prayer meetings in the center of the city. Muslim and Christian leaders would go on television to implore people to work together peacefully. On one of our visits, Christian leaders invited us to join them at the central mosque to share with the Muslims in eating the delicacies as they broke their Ramadan fast.

At the gathering they asked about ways I have been engaged in building bridges of peace between Muslims and Christians. I gave them English copies of *A Muslim and a Christian in Dialogue.* They immediately decided to translate and publish the book in Indonesian. About two years later the book was ready for a launching. Grace and I had the privilege of being present. About

3. This account of seeking reconciliation in Solo, Indonesia, has been rather widely circulated in various media. In 2008 I wrote an article for the *International Bulletin of Missionary Research* in which this account and other accounts at peacemaking were included. See David W. Shenk, "The Gospel of Reconciliation within the Wrath of Nations," *International Bulletin of Missionary Research,* 31, no. 1 (2008): 3–6, 8–9. The bulletin has approved my using an adaptation of the Solo account in this book.

eighty leaders participated. A lunch was served and speeches were given. I shared that I am an emissary of the peace of the Messiah, who forgave those who crucified him and who empowers his disciples to love as he loved. It was an excellent event, contributing positively to the commitment to cultivate peaceful relations.

Then, to my surprise, we were taken to the Hezbollah command center.[4] The commander had ten thousand militia under his authority. This group had sometimes exercised atrocities against churches. We were escorted into the headquarters with a phalanx of militia escorts along our path. We sat in a large half circle, with the militia officers sitting with us to complete the circle.

They said, "Welcome! We will explain our mission. We kill our enemies and fight to defend the integrity of Islam against all threats."

We asked if we may respond. They granted permission. "This kind of mission creates more enemies," I responded. "Jesus showed another way. That is to forgive one's enemies. When we forgive our enemies, we have no enemies."

They were obviously quite astonished at this novel idea for dealing with enemies.

Then the pastor who had arranged this meeting gave the commander a copy of *Dialogue*. The commander paged through it. He shed tears. The pastor was sitting beside the commander and reached over to pat him on the shoulder. The shoulder patting was saying, "We have forgiven you." At one time the commander and his militia had been engaged in acts that brought suffering to some Christian communities. The commander explained that he was touched by the spirit of the book, which respects everyone, even those with whom one disagrees. He said if everyone in Indonesia practiced the spirit of *A Muslim and a Christian in Dialogue*, Indonesia would be transformed. He asked for fifty copies of the book, one for each of his officers. The gathering concluded with an ample meal, with much opportunity for the thirty Christians present to intermingle and converse with the militia.

---

4. *Hezbollah* means "the Party of God." A well-known Hezbollah functions as a Shi'a political/military force in Lebanon. The militia group we met with in Solo, Indonesia, is a Sunni political/militia group.

Peacemaking of this kind demands focus and intention. Two years earlier, the pastor had gone to the home of the militia commander and asked to have a cup of tea together. After making an explicit threat, the commander begrudgingly accepted. The pastor was not intimidated, and thereafter went to the home of the commander again and again for tea. Slowly, trusting relations developed. This was the first tentative step, drinking tea together.

Then the pastor invited the commander and his militia officers to fly to Banda Aceh to work with pastors who were also flying to this region where the 2004 tsunami had caused enormous devastation several years earlier. The Hezbollah officers accepted the invitation, so for some days these two communities worked together in reconstruction, even though they had a long history of mistrust and conflict. Amazingly, the pastor slept in the same room with the very commander who some months before had threatened him. They became friends. One evening, sitting at the cooking fire, the commander began to weep. He commented that his heart was melting within him as he considered how he had related to Christians. He was now learning they were godly and generous, and in fact were helping the Muslims of Banda Aceh, not doing them any harm.

The pastor refers to this approach to peacemaking as a "dialogue of praxis." The dialogue of working together is probably more fruitful than the dialogue of words. It is in working together that we really learn to know one another and that genuine friendship can flourish.

The Muslim and Christian peacebuilders in Solo are committed to equipping leaders for the task of developing a peaceful civil society. They have acquired scholarships for several to study at Eastern Mennonite University in its Summer Peacebuilding Institute. This university in Harrisonburg, Virginia, in the United States, offers programs in peacemaking that attract leaders from around the world who are serving in conflict situations. When Grace and I were in Solo recently, we met several of the trainees. They spoke highly of the value of the institute in helping to equip peacemakers for the Solo context. Wise is the church, mosque, or any local community who identifies the person or people of peace from within their community. It is also wise to provide these peacemakers with insights and skills that are helpful in peacemaking.

The churches in Solo are growing, for there is much interest in Jesus and the peace he offers. They need more land, as well as building permits. In many areas of Indonesia, it is difficult to get such permits. However, in Solo, the Hezbollah commander is committed to working with the pastor to acquire permits for building churches. He also notifies the pastor if he is aware of any brewing challenges to the peace, such as militants planning a church burning. In that case, the commander and the pastor work together to extinguish the flames.

I asked the pastor how he accounts for this transformation. With a mischievous twinkle, he said, "Lots of cups of tea!"

Then he added, "This is the work of the Holy Spirit. We are not capable of building these peacemaking bridges. We flow in prayer."

Engaging jihadism

Muslim militancy and jihadism are of great concern to mainstream Muslims, as well as non-Muslims. This is not only the historic conflict between Shi'a and Sunni Islam; there is also the multiplication of jihadist militia like the Hezbollah in Central Java described above. The jihadists are often encouraged by visions of a purist Islam they think modern secularist Muslims have abandoned. Therefore, much of the jihadists' anger is directed against fellow Muslims. How can these movements be addressed?

There are ample verses within the Qur'an inviting Muslims into peacemaking ways.[5] This is especially true of the passages in the Qur'an proclaimed during the twelve years Muhammad was in Mecca without access to political or military power. The portions of the Qur'an condoning violence that the jihadists look to for divine support were mostly proclaimed in Medina after Muhammad had acquired political and military power. They are proclamations denouncing those who take land or property from Muslims. It is noteworthy that these "sword" verses are

---

5. Qur'an: *Maida* (The Table Spread): surah 5:16; *Nisaa* (Women): surah 4:128; *Hadid* (Iron): surah 57:25.

proclaimed as a response to provocation or threats to the *umma*.[6] The Hezbollah in Solo probably represented Muslim concerns about the challenges of maintaining a pure Islam in the pluralistic environment of Indonesia. They were also concerned about the significant growth of the church.

Western militancy also needs to be addressed. For example, how can the phenomenon of drone attacks be challenged? The occasional attacks spawn massive paranoia in some regions of northern Pakistan; no one knows when the next stealth rocket will silently attack. What is the role of a follower of Jesus in times like these?

Several years ago a companion and I went to the U.S. State Department to meet with the leadership of the Iran section. Our plea was to open conversations with the Iranians. The same day, Douglas Johnston, president and founder of the International Center for Religion and Diplomacy, was speaking in a forum on Islamic militancy. He observed that this threat is dangerous but cannot be dealt with militarily. He asserted that a military solution simply multiplies those ready to join the jihad. Johnston also insisted that the challenge cannot be addressed philosophically, but only theologically.[7] This peace emissary described his meetings with Taliban leaders in northern Pakistan. He and his team would discuss with the Taliban some of the peacemaking passages of the Qur'an.

Johnston's talk reminded me of the peacemaking efforts of a Christian friend with the militant youth fighting in Somalia. When he is able to meet with leaders, he commences with a study of the Qur'an, pointing out that every *surah* in the Qur'an except one begins: "In the name of God the compassionate, the merciful." Then he asks whether these youth are living compassionately and what it means to be a youth movement committed to mercy. He and his team have been welcomed and respected.

---

6. Qur'an: *Baqara* (The Heifer): surah 2:190-91, 193.
7. Douglas Johnston and Brian Cox, "Faith-Based Diplomacy and Preventive Engagement," in *Faith-Based Diplomacy: Trumping Realpolitik*, ed. Douglas Johnston (New York: Oxford University Press, 2002), 11–32.

Healing for the nations

In August 2014 several dozen churches were burned by jihadists in Egypt, when the country was in the throes of a season of political turmoil. The next Sunday, congregations gathered in the ashes of their burned churches. Children stood around the congregations meeting for worship. The children held high banners that proclaimed forgiveness for those who had burned their churches. On the outer edges of the gatherings, Muslim neighbors formed a circle around the Christians in worship, to protect them should the perpetrators of the church burnings seek to disturb the gatherings. People throughout Egypt were touched by this spirit of forgiveness and reaching out for reconciliation.[8]

Mohammed Abu-Nimer, whose roots are in Palestine, describes the culture of peaceful transformation that can develop when Christians and Muslims work and live together. He names this culture "Islamicate Society"[9]—a Muslim culture influenced by peace themes within Christian communities. Muslim peace themes and Christian peacemaking meet. This is what Egypt observed in the wake of the church burnings. Recall that Jesus referred to the peacemaking role of his disciples as "salt," "light," and "leaven."

Recently several dozen Muslims and Christians in Philadelphia had a long evening of dynamic encounter discussing the civil war unfolding in Syria. At the end of the evening several commented, "This has been good for our mosque congregation, to talk together in a civil spirit about these issues we feel so deeply about. Having guests with us was helpful!" I believe that evening all participants experienced the fruit of the Islamicate civil society Abu-Nimer is describing.

In times like these, we recognize in new ways that the power center of history is the man on a cross who forgives those who have crucified him. In his forgiveness, the cycles of violence and retribution are broken, for he absorbs the hostility, he forgives, and he embraces those who have been in conflict. That man and

---

8. Anne Zaki, "Is the Arab Spring the Arab Christian's Fall?" (January Series lecture, Calvin College, Grand Rapids, MI, January 27, 2014).
9. Mohammed Abu-Nimer, *Nonviolence and Peace Building in Islam: Theory and Practice* (Gainesville: University of Florida Press, 2003), 164.

the community of reconciliation committed to him are the hope of the world. It is urgent for those who have taken his name to genuinely seek peace and pursue it.

In traditional Muslim societies around the world, covenants of peace involve the sacrifice of a lamb or a ram. This is especially true within the mystical stream of theology known as Sufism. These Muslims seek to find a way to experience God. In this context, Paul's letter to the Ephesians makes a lot of sense. Paul writes, "But now in Christ Jesus you who once were far away have been brought near through the blood of Christ. For he himself is our peace, who has made the two groups one and has destroyed the barrier, the dividing wall of hostility."[10]

Wherever the walls are going up, the mission of the church is to seek ways to partner with the Holy Spirit and the people of peace in bringing down those walls. We need to repent of any inclination to be wall-building dividers and commit to being peacemaking bridge builders.

Questions for discussion

1. Consider the specific steps Indonesian peacemakers took in their engagement with the militant Muslim Hezbollah.
2. What are some specific steps you could take to cultivate trusting relations between Muslims and Christians? For example, are there any universities within reach of your home? Could youth in your church find ways to invite Muslim university students into homes in your community?
3. What is your response to the approach of Douglas Johnston in reaching out to the Taliban in Pakistan?
4. Notice how these peacemaking initiatives all began small and hardly noticed, like drinking tea with the Hezbollah commander. What are some ways you or your church could plant little seeds of peacemaking?

---

10. Bible: Ephesians 2:13-14.

CHAPTER 11
Partner with the Person of Peace

Every day our newspapers report on acts of terror. At a Christian-Muslim dialogue in New Delhi, several students approached me and commented, "We are perplexed. You are an American Christian and yet you are a person of peace. We thought American Christians are terrorists."

In the previous chapter, we observed that terrorism and jihadism are global concerns, and gave special attention to cultivating peacemaking relations with jihadists. In this chapter, we look at specific examples of a strategy of peacemaking that is informed by the "person of peace."[1]

When I speak in churches and the time for questions comes, I can be sure that one of the first questions will be, "What are the roots of Muslim terrorism? How should we respond to terrorism?"

The definition and roots of terrorism

Terrorism is difficult to define. It was U.S. president George W. Bush who popularized the notion of the "war on terrorism." In this book I use *jihadism* as the Muslim use of violence to defend the house of Islam within the bounds of Islamic theology and mainstream Muslim leadership. I use *terrorism* as violence that the credible Muslim *ulama* consider to be outside the constraints of legitimate jihad. For example, suicide bombings that

---

1. Bible: see Luke 10:5-6.

kill innocents are acts of terrorism and go beyond the bounds that the Qur'an dictates for combatants in wartime.

I also recognize that what non-Islamic powers consider to be legitimate acts of violence might be viewed as terrorism by innocents on the ground. The controversy over using drones to kill "terrorist" leaders is a case in point. So the questions and perplexity about terrorism come from all sides. The terrorists choose their directions because they believe their way is right and in fulfillment of the will of God. They believe their violent acts are necessary in order to bring about good. We decry their misinterpretation of God who is the merciful and compassionate one.

Surely the men who flew the planes into the Twin Towers believed they were doing the will of God. The terrorist attacks of 9/11 are imprinted on memories around the world. The wars that followed have sown seeds of grievance that run deep. The roots of the grievances are many; we cannot list them.

I will comment on two dimensions of grievance and terrorism. The first comes to us through the pen of Sayyid Qutb, an Egyptian. He came to the United States for studies in 1949 just after the state of Israel was created. His two years in the United States were lonely. He yearned for friends with whom he could commiserate. He returned to Egypt believing Western civilization was decadent, materialistic, and doomed.

The formation of the state of Israel during his time in the United States was for him justification of a deep grievance. He believed it was supremely unjust for Israel to acquire land that Palestinians had occupied for many centuries. He was disillusioned especially by the North American churches that supported this injustice. He was embittered, and consequently his ideology became increasingly anti-Christian. In his thinking, Christians were infidels, a designation Muslim *ulama* have traditionally resisted.

Back in Egypt, Qutb became heavily involved with the Muslim Brotherhood and was subsequently imprisoned for over a decade because of his apocalyptic solutions for Westernized countries. His solution was the destruction of the whole modern enterprise and a return to the purist faith of Islam. He wrote prolifically, especially in his prison years. His thirty-volume *The Shade of the Qur'an* and his compendium, *Milestones*, have powerfully influenced the directions jihadist terrorism has taken. Although he was executed in 1966, Qutb's death did not quell the influence of his writings on terroristic ideology. His books are the bread and butter of modern terrorism such as that of Al Qaida.[2] I would expect that Qutb's writings might have contributed to the ideology that motivated the Boston Marathon bombers.[3]

Another influential stream that attracts regular press coverage is the Taliban. It is noteworthy that in their early beginnings, the Taliban were orphans. They were cared for in orphanages in Pakistan. These orphanages were developed as a compassionate response for the huge humanitarian crisis at the time of the separation of India and Pakistan in 1947. The boys, housed in orphanages that were male-run, grew up with little contact with mother figures. Theirs was a man's world. These emotionally wounded children grew up with little contact with the wider world. In time, they emerged with a mission that was different from that of the wider Muslim society in which they lived. They were insulated from the dynamism of the wider Pakistani society. So whenever I hear "Taliban," I think of a person who at one time was an orphan, a person who needs compassion.

I do not mean to suggest there is a straight line connecting the Taliban or Sayyid Qutb and terrorism. I am simply opening the window into some dimensions of terrorist realities.

How, then, can Christians go about peacemaking within contexts formed by these kinds of ideologies? That is also a question Muslims ask. As I listen to Muslim theologians and leaders around the world, I hear much concern about distorted interpretations of Islam that ignore the many affirmations of peacemaking in the Qur'an. And how should disciples of Jesus or Muslims committed to peace engage Western leaders who believe a military solution is the best solution?

The grievances driving terroristic acts, such as those of suicide bombers, are complex. Just as American Christians decry any link between the Christian faith and the murderous Ku Klux

---

2. For a scholarly exploration of Sayyid Qutb's ideology, see Neal Robinson, "Sayyid Qutb's Attitude Towards Christianity: Surah 9.29-35 in Fi Zilal Al-Qur'an," in *Islamic Interpretations of Christianity,* ed. Lloyd Ridgeon (Surrey, UK: Curzon, 2001): 159–78.
3. On April 15, 2013, bombings killed and maimed participants in the annual Boston Marathon. Those responsible seem to have been influenced by jihadist indoctrination.

Klan, so also are most Muslims horrified when suicide bombers claim to be practicing Islam. Would a Muslim or a Christian who believes in the compassion of God kill innocent people? The issues are theological!

In my conversations about peacemaking with Muslims, I find that Jesus quickly occupies the center of the conversation. This is because the approach of Jesus the Messiah to peacemaking turns our understandings of God upside down. Jesus is radical!

A former jihadist speaks out for peace

This idea of a radical Jesus imbued our breakfast conversation recently. We were enjoying a lavish breakfast in the home of Indonesian friends in their Jakarta home. A gray-bearded man we had never met before was across the table from us. During a fleeting lull in the conversation, I interjected, "I have heard you are a man of peace."

Grace and I were astounded at his answer. In a flash he vehemently exclaimed, "No! I am not a man of peace. I am a violent man. I was one of those who planned and implemented the Bali bombings.[4] How can anyone say I am a man of peace? I am a violent man! I am not a man of peace. I am a terrorist.

"My friends," he exclaimed, "Jesus is the peace! I planned violent crimes, believing violence is the way to bring about God's will on earth. Then I met Jesus. He turned me all around. I am still a Muslim. But I am a Jesus-centered Muslim. I tell you, Jesus really does matter! Read the Sermon on the Mount. We all need Jesus.

"Without sacrifice there can be no peace. We know that in our traditional religions. Even within Islam there is the traditional feast of sacrifice. These sacrifices are signs pointing to Jesus and his sacrifice. He is the reconciling sacrifice. He is our peace."[5]

For the next hour he described how Jesus had met him and turned him around. Jesus opened his eyes to see that the jihadist approach to establishing the will of God is disaster. Jesus demonstrates peacemaking. All over the world where people are embracing the Jesus alternative, there is forgiveness and new life.

---

4. On October 1, 2005, bombers attacked a resort in Bali, killing twenty and injuring 129.
5. Qur'an: *Saffat* (Those Ranged in Ranks): surah 37:107; Bible: Luke 22:19-20; Ephesians 2:13-19.

This peacemaker recognizes that within his soul there lurks the seed of violence. He has come to the unshakable conviction that Jesus is the alternative. He travels across Indonesia urging jihadists to turn to Jesus, who brings healing and not death.

Planting seeds of peace

Christians committed to peacemaking will discover there are Muslims who are eager to become allies in peacemaking. The account of Muhammad going from Mecca to the town of Taif is an encouragement to Muslims seeking peaceful ways to deal with those who abuse them. At a time of great discouragement after his wife's death, Muhammad visited Taif and was stoned and severely treated. He was forced to leave the town and return to Mecca, where he was also frequently maltreated. His response was to find solace in God and to have the confidence that retribution belongs to God.[6]

In the Taif experience, Muhammad demonstrated the qualities that are essential in the person of peace. Jesus commanded his disciples to look for the person of peace. The person of peace in a community can influence the community in peacemaking ways. Only the most imaginative Christian peacemakers would have considered a Hezbollah militia commander as a partner in peacemaking, as described in the previous chapter.

The pastor in the account of peacemaking in Solo has explained to me his approach to intercommunity peacemaking. First, he engages the Muslim and Christian leaders who are genuinely committed to developing bridges for peacemaking between the two communities. These leaders are all persons of peace. They meet together regularly and think imaginatively of approaches to peacemaking. They are also committed to moving beyond their circle to find ways to engage militant Muslims—or militant Christians, for that matter.

Peacemaking Muslims are inspired by the reference to Cain and Abel in the Qur'an. Cain is coming to kill Abel, who cries out to God that he would rather die than use his sword to protect himself against the weapon wielded by Cain. So Abel dies

---

6. Qur'an: *Jinn* (Spirits): surah 72:1-28.

rather than kill his brother. God commends Abel for his refusal to use the sword.[7] There are many such insights that form the commitments of peacemaking Muslims. As I mentioned previously, probably the most notable peace sign in the Qur'an is that every *surah*, except the first, opens with the expression "In the name of God the merciful and the compassionate." Also significant is the Muslim greeting, which is an affirmation of the blessing of peace upon one's brother or sister. These are values peacemaking Christians can identify with.

It was such peace-loving themes that began to open the door for the Hezbollah commander to become a participant in the peacemaking circle in Solo. Moderate Muslims who knew the commander helped to facilitate those tea-drinking encounters. They encouraged the pastor to take this initiative. Those who knew the commander hoped that within his militancy there was a heart committed to peacemaking. He and his colleagues had the long-term goal of establishing the peace of Islam in Central Java.

The mission of the pastor was to encourage the commander to begin to view his peacemaking commitments as including non-Muslims. That was a tremendous stretch. But in time he had become a person of peace, encouraging both the Muslims and Christians to desist from violent confrontation against one another. In fact, one of the militia officers has become a believer in the Prince of Peace and is now proclaiming the peace of the Messiah in Central Java.

The pastor now has an even broader vision. He is working with the Hezbollah officers to identify leaders within the terrorist communities who have been engaged in atrocities such as suicide bombings. His hope is that through engagement a transformation may occur that would sow peacemaking seeds. His commitment is to engage not only militants but terrorists in cultivating peacemaking. This is slow work. It requires three *P*s: persistence, patience, and prayer.

The broad society-transforming vision for peacemaking is remarkable. The seed is first planted within the leaders who are genuinely committed to peacemaking. These are the persons of peace. Then these leaders take the baton further by seeking

---

7. Qur'an: *Maida* (The Table Spread): surah 5:30, 34.

persons of peace within the militant Muslim communities. Then they work with the militant Muslim persons of peace to engage the terroristic communities. The biblical Scriptures command us to "seek peace and pursue it."[8] This kind of peacemaking requires imaginative persistence.

This is what two peacemakers in Nigeria are doing—pursuing peace within regions of the country rent with violence between Christians and Muslims. Both Christians and Muslims have suffered immensely. It is in this volatile context that Rev. Dr. James Mavel Wuye and Imam Dr. Muhammad Nurayan Ashafa have developed alternative peacemaking approaches. These men were leaders in their respective communities. They fanned the flames of mistrust and violence.

Then, amazingly, they both began to realize the futility of their violence. They repented and reached out to each other in friendship-building ways. They developed a video sharing their experience in reconciliation and urging others to follow their example. These two men, an imam and a pastor, have become persons of peace seeking the peace of communities across Nigeria. They travel together, heralding the invitation across the country to desist from violence and build bridges of trust and reconciliation.[9]

An ambassador of the Prince of Peace

Another peacemaker is from East Africa and served as an apostle of the peace of Christ in Somalia, Kenya, and the United States. He is Ahmed Ali Haile.[10] He was a Muslim living in the central regions of Somalia. At fifteen years of age he met Christians for the first time when he was ill with malaria and admitted to a Christian mission hospital. As he was recovering, a Christian nurse gave him a Bible to read. During the next two years he read through the Bible twice and then went to the home of the missionary doctor who directed the hospital.

---

8. Bible: 1 Peter 3:11.
9. David W. Shenk, "Christian-Muslim Conflict Zones and Possibilities for Peace," in *Evangelical Peacemakers: Gospel Engagement in a War-Torn World*, ed. David P. Gushee (Eugene, OR: Cascade Books, 2013), 59–68.
10. Ahmed Ali Haile as told to David W. Shenk, *Teatime in Mogadishu: My Journey as a Peace Ambassador in the World of Islam* (Harrisonburg, VA: Herald Press, 2011).

He said forthrightly, "I have decided to become a believer in the Messiah."

The doctor did not mince words. "This might mean you will be put out of your home. Scholarships for study will probably not come your way, and your friends might abandon you. It could be someone will believe you should die for this decision."

Ahmed responded, "I have thought carefully about the cost. I have decided to follow Jesus the Messiah."

So began Ahmed's journey as an ambassador of the Messiah, the Prince of Peace. He invested his life as a peacemaker, with special focus on Somali-speaking peoples. Nevertheless, he served wherever his gifts in peacemaking were requested. Often his peacemaking commitments occurred within contexts where he was under threat, for peacemakers are considered dangerous by those who are committed to violent alternatives. On one occasion when he was working at some delicate peace negotiations in Somalia, opponents of the peace process shot a rocket at the house where he was staying. He lost his leg in the attack. In fact, he nearly lost his life. Yet he persisted in the confident hope that in God's own time, the peace of Christ would prevail.

When living in Somalia and later in Kenya, he and his wife, Martha, lived in a house with a tree in the yard. This tree was nicknamed "Ahmed's tree." Once a week, clan leaders as well as Muslim *ulama* would gather under Ahmed's tree for conversations on peacemaking in their troubled homeland, Somalia. So this peacemaker's influence permeated Somali society at a time when counteracting forces strongly opposed reconciliation.

Ahmed was a believer in Jesus the Messiah. His colleagues knew that he believed only the cross could deal with the roots of conflict. All other levels of peacemaking did not really address the core issues rooted in our sinfulness and alienation from God and from one another. Christ, in his crucifixion and resurrection through the empowerment of the Holy Spirit, brings about a new creation and authentic forgiveness and reconciliation. This is what Ahmed believed and what he confessed as he counseled and shared with those leaders gathering at his home week by week.

Networking for peace

Most of those leaders were not believers in the Messiah. They sang from a different sheet of music. So Ahmed, as a highly respected peace negotiator, would work with the clan and religious leaders at whatever level they were ready to accept. Some were committed to an Islamic approach. So Ahmed worked with those leaders in thinking through ways Islamic approaches to peacemaking could address the challenges of Somalia. A key theme was the *umma*. All Muslims participate in the *umma,* the universal Muslim community of peace. So if Muslim community identity was the *umma*, then clan-based loyalties needed to give primary allegiance to the universal community of worldwide Muslims.

Ahmed also found helpful themes in the traditional pre-Islamic societies. Especially significant were the themes that sought restoration. Forgiveness and restoration trumped retribution in traditional pre-Islamic society. In the traditional culture, when there is conflict, the elders meet to determine the source of the conflict and then the steps needed to restore the person who has erred. He will likely give some camels to those he has offended. Then the clan or person who has received the camels in restitution will probably offer a camel back to the offender so he can kill the camel and invite everyone to a grand feast of restoration. Both parties enjoy a camel feast together. In the midst of all this is a covenant of peace for all parties to participate in. The covenant is sealed through the offering of an animal, with feasting accompanying the restoration. The feasting brings closure. Peace has returned.

The peace is sealed by God himself. The traditional name for God in the Somali language is *Bar Waaq*, meaning "the God of blessing." In fact, the place where restoration and reconciliation has happened is *Barwako*, "the place where the blessing of God is present."[11]

Ahmed believed the traditional societies carried significant biblical themes wherein restoration was significant. He also drew upon the rich lore of proverbs related to peacemaking. One proverb he often referred to tells of a woman carrying a basket of figs on her head when she meets her enemies on the road. She gives

11. Ibid., 89–92.

her basket of figs to her enemy and goes on her way without figs, for she has given the figs as a gift. Her gift has transformed her enemies into her friends.

Peacemaking in Tanzania

We have observed that partners in peacemaking need to address the obstacles. I have also observed that peacemakers need to be proactive. That was my experience when meeting with president Jakaya Kikwete of Tanzania, a Muslim. Friends suggested he might meet with me to consider proactive steps for enhancing Christian-Muslim peacemaking in Tanzania. When I stopped by the State House, he stepped out of a cabinet meeting so we could meet. He had two requests. First, he needed one thousand copies of *A Muslim and a Christian in Dialogue* in Swahili for distribution to key Muslim and Christian leaders. Second, he asked me to work with a team he would appoint to convene a peacemaking gathering of key Muslim and Christian leaders across Tanzania.

The gathering was held in April 2012. About 150 leaders participated, and each was given a free copy of *A Muslim and a Christian in Dialogue*, courtesy of the president. We organized the dialogue around exploring various themes concerning Abraham, who was called by God to be a blessing to all nations. A highlight was Muslim leaders sharing what they appreciated about Christians and Christians what they appreciated about Muslims. Then, in another caucus, the respective groups talked about ways that they could bless and encourage one another.

Then, in the midst of it all, there was a heated exchange. I prayed! Others prayed! It seemed the conference would explode in shambles. The issue was a push from some of the Muslims for Tanzania to become a member of the Council of Islamic Countries. The church leadership was strongly opposed. Tanzania is constitutionally a secular state, and separation of church and state is cherished by the churches. Church leaders believed that joining a global network of Muslim countries would undermine the secularist nature of Tanzania. Thanks to the strong leadership of the Muslim and Christian cochairs, the storm passed and we concluded the two-day event in peace.

A few months after the event, there were several violent episodes between Muslims and Christians. Several leaders who had participated in the dialogue conference met together on national television to share about the amicable dialogue they had participated in. They encouraged the whole nation to emulate the peacemaking spirit of their leaders.

We cannot overstate the necessity and significance of proactive peacemaking. Muslims and Christians need to work at many levels in preserving the peace!

Informal peacebuilding relationships

Although I now live in North America, I experience a generous peacemaking spirit among Muslims living in the West. I have many conversations with the imams in the mosques I visit. All are persons of peace in their various ways. One leader of a mosque has time and again given us a full meal when we visit. He does this at his own expense. As many as thirty people participate in these meals. Our host spreads a long cloth across the floor of the mosque, and we sit in rows, eating our fill. The Muslims and Christians intermingle as we eat and converse.

On one occasion, the mosque leader and I had a heated disagreement revolving around the issue of the freedom of choice to believe or not believe. The next time we met, the feast was spread again, and the mosque leader welcomed us by extending an apology for his spirit and comments the time before. He is a man of peace!

Often our hosts begin the conversation with prayer. Sometimes I lead in the closing prayer by reciting the prayer Jesus taught us to pray. It begins by addressing God as our Father in heaven. Pertinent to our quest for peacemaking is the next statement in the prayer: "Thy kingdom come, thy will be done, on earth as it is in heaven." And then in the middle of the prayer: "Forgive our sins as we forgive the sins of others against us!" This is indeed a peacemaking prayer that I return to again and again as I meet with Christians and Muslims in dialogue.

Youth and children have a special role in peacemaking. The normal routines of school, for example, often put Muslim and Christian students together in the classroom and playground.

They learn to play together; sometimes they argue and perhaps even fight with each other. They are learning to be a community.

In many areas of the world, Muslim students make special efforts to enroll in Christian schools. That was our experience in Somalia; in fact, graduates of our schools were considered to be peacemakers. They were nicknamed the "Mennonites." These mostly Muslim "Mennonites" have been at the forefront of peacemaking efforts in Somalia.

A Pakistani once told me, "I will never speak condescendingly of Christians, for in Pakistan I went to a Christian high school. I got an excellent education, and more than that I developed lasting friendships with Christians. We Muslims were respected by the Christian students. I shall always be grateful for that experience."

Don't let mistakes discourage you

Sometimes we fumble, and instead of peacemaking we create walls. I will share one example which should make it clear that my wife and I are not experts in this journey; we will always be learners.

Our next-door neighbors are Muslim immigrants. Shortly after they arrived, we had them over for dessert and an evening of getting acquainted. Then we invited them to send their children with us to summer Bible school. The mother made it clear that they would not want their children attending a Bible school; when their children are mature, she said, they will have freedom to choose their faith. She did not want her children to be indoctrinated by Christians. The conversation was congenial.

Then came Christmas. We have the practice of taking a colorful paper plate of homemade cookies to each of our neighbors. We usually sing a short carol as we give them this token gift. Muslims recognize Jesus as an endowed prophet whose birth Christians celebrate on Christmas. So we went to their door as we do to all our other neighbors. They were troubled by the song and rejected the gift of cookies, pointing out that they were struggling to keep their children away from Christmas celebrations. Our gift and the brief carol were highly offensive.

We are praying and seeking a way to restore relations. Shortly after this incident, I was traveling to their homeland. I offered to take anything for relatives they might want to send with me. This turned out to be impractical, but offering to take a package was a small first step in restoring relationship. Our neighbor and Grace recently waved to each other across the road that divides our properties. We believe we are on the way!

Most Muslims we know would appreciate the gesture of goodwill the cookies and song suggested. At Christmas, a number of my Muslim acquaintances send us Christmas cards, often with angels announcing the birth of Jesus, a theme that is also in the Qur'an. But we have not been sufficiently tuned in to the fears and challenges our neighbors are experiencing. Their commitment to passing on their faith to their children, while living in an environment quite influenced by Christian beliefs and practices, has been difficult.

I share this offense so you are aware that mistakes are part of the journey.

Ahmed, the one-legged peacemaker

Ahmed often said that only the cross goes to the root of the matter and deals with the source of violent conflict. He felt all other solutions were superficial, but he would work at peacemaking at whatever depth people were ready to go. So he worked with Somali clan leaders as they identified the values of peacemaking within their traditional societies. He did the same with themes in the Muslim faith. Yet he returned again and again to his central theme: in the Messiah crucified and risen, God offers the grace of forgiveness, reconciliation, and restoration.

After Ahmed received a wooden leg, his presence could be heard quite loudly as he walked with the wood banging on the floor. One of his seminary professors in the United States told me that on one occasion, he heard the thump of Ahmed's leg coming up the hall. At that time, Ahmed and their family were living in East Africa, so the thump signaled that Ahmed must be briefly visiting the States. His professor opened the door to welcome Ahmed.

They greeted each other, and Ahmed went straight to his point. He said, "Authentic peace is centered in the cross of Jesus Christ. If we teach peacemaking without the cross, we are missing the heart of the matter. Only the cross goes to the root causes of our broken relationships. Remember! Goodbye!"

Ahmed left, heading for the exit, his wooden leg thumping all the way down the hallway.

Questions for discussion
1. Describe approaches to peacemaking that Muslims who are faithful to their scriptures will embrace.
2. What is a distinctive gift the church offers in peacemaking?
3. Consider the way Ahmed Haile wove together different approaches to peacemaking. What is your response to Ahmed's approach to peacemaking in a Muslim environment?
4. Imagine Ahmed sitting under his tree every Thursday with elders of his clan and leaders of the mosque, talking about peacemaking among the Somali people. Imagine the ideas they might share. Remember that most were Muslims.
5. What is your response to Ahmed's conviction that "only the cross goes to the heart of peacemaking"?

CHAPTER 12
Commend Christ

I once rode in a taxi in Chicago with a Muslim driver from Pakistan. I introduced myself as a Christian. Immediately he plunged into a critique of Christian three-god theology. The conversation became animated. It was to be a forty-five-minute drive.

About sixty minutes later, he discovered he had driven me far from the right address. He did not charge me for extra miles.

The taxi driver's riveting interest in the God discussion in a taxi is typical of most Muslims I meet. Muslims cherish opportunities to talk about God. This means there are often open doors to converse about faith.

Ahmed's awakening interest in the gospel

Recall that Ahmed was thrilled when a Christian nurse gave him a Bible to read when he was ill with malaria in a mission hospital. He was grateful. Here he finally had in his hands the Scripture that contains the Torah and other Scriptures that God has revealed. Later, he learned that the whole Bible is accepted by Christians as the Word of God. However, the first step in realizing the message of the Bible was reading the Torah that the Qur'an proclaims is revealed by God.

Ahmed often commented to me, "Islam is not the gospel. But how can I be critical of Islam when God used Islam to lead me to the Messiah through the Bible? It was in the mosque I learned from the kindly imam that there are other scriptures besides the Qur'an that God has revealed. I am grateful for those evenings in the mosque where the imam opened my heart to quest for the other scriptures revealed by God. I am also grateful for my godly family, who helped me face a spiritual trajectory that in time led me to the Messiah."

What is the gospel?

There are many such signs of the gospel in Islam. However, the signs are not the gospel itself. When driving to a destination, I will see signs pointing me to the destination. If I stop at a sign, I will never arrive at the destination. I need to actually go to the destination indicated by the sign. Many of my Muslim acquaintances assert with great conviction that they believe in the Torah, Psalms, Gospels, and all the holy writings, but they never read these Scriptures. This is like stopping at the sign along the highway but never proceeding to the designated destination.

In the Bible, the destination God intends is salvation. I believe the soul of God's gift of salvation is best stated in one sentence: "For God so loved the world that he gave his one and only Son, that whoever believes in him shall not perish but have eternal life."[1]

In contrast, Ahmed's mother would recite a passage from the Qur'an four hundred times every night before falling asleep. This was the *Ikhlas*, known as the "Purity of Faith": "Say: 'He is God, The One and Only; God the Eternal, Absolute; He begetteth not, Nor is he begotten; And there is none like unto him.'"[2] Muslims consider this passage to be the soul of the Qur'an. It is a call to surrender to the will of God.

Christians also are called to surrender to God. In Jesus, we meet God as the one who loves us and who redeems and saves. The gospel is like an African stool with a seat and three legs: the seat is the life and teachings of Jesus; the legs are the incarnation, the crucifixion, and the resurrection of the Messiah. The salvation that Christians proclaim is centered in these four dimensions of the life and mission of Jesus the Messiah.

---

1. Bible: John 3:16.
2. Qur'an: *Ikhlas* (The Purity of Faith): surah 112.

The importance of access to the Bible

A young mother in central Asia shared her pilgrimage into faith in the Messiah with my wife, Grace. She explained, "Someone gave me a New Testament. I placed it on a shelf. But later I tucked this little book into my bag as I went to the hospital for the difficult delivery of my child. The baby was born during a blizzard, with my husband stranded miles from home. As I lay in my hospital bed, I reached into my bag for the little book. I began to read. I was astonished. Then Jesus revealed himself to me. I believed right there in the hospital. When I returned home, neighbors saw my face was glowing. They wondered what had happened to me to fill me with so much joy. I shared with them the good news that Jesus the Messiah had met me in my hospital bed. I named my baby Sunshine in remembrance of the sunshine in my soul."

We recognize that not all Muslims receive the Bible with the appreciation Sunshine's mother did. However, Paul reminds us that those who never read the written Bible will nevertheless read the lives of believers in Jesus.

Paul writes that believers are a "letter . . . known and read by everyone. You show that you are a letter from Christ."[3]

In Somalia, the illiterate cook in one of our boarding schools went to the storage room for supplies. On his brief walk he heard the headmaster's wife singing. He knew she sang because of joy. Her joy was the letter from heaven leading him to a commitment to Jesus the Messiah as his Savior and Lord.

A Muslim quest for Islamic signs of truth

Christians are grateful when Muslims follow a sign of truth, such as the Qur'anic assertion that Jesus is a sign to all nations, which leads then to the gospel. We are also aware that Muslims scrutinize the Bible to look for signs, such as dreams, to establish the faith of Islam. For example, I have commented on the belief of many Muslims that when Jesus promised the coming of the Holy Spirit, he was really promising the coming of Muhammad. Muslims believe that Islam rounds out all previous revelation, and so they look for proofs that Islam is the true and final faith of humankind.

---

3. Bible: 2 Corinthians 3:2-3.

When we invite Muslims to consider the gospel, we meet the reality that Muslims are often positioned to invite the Christian to consider Islam. They will ground that invitation on signs of "truth" that establish the truth of Islam. That reality means that both the witnessing church and the witnessing *umma* believe they have a truth to tell. That is okay! It is one reason that Christian-Muslim dialogue is much more than a quiet parlor exchange of ideas.

The messianic mystery

Jesus is the mystery person of the Qur'an. Many signs surround his personhood. Born of a virgin; the Messiah; a sign to all nations; miracle worker; fulfillment of the scriptures; coming again; the Word of God; the Spirit of God; without sin; good news. Any of these signs explored with an appreciation of New Testament revelation would help open the door into discovering Jesus the Messiah.

One quite amazing sign in regard to Jesus is found in the *surah* known as "The Table Spread" (*Maida*). The disciples of Jesus beseech him to send a table from heaven with food so that they can eat of its provisions and be satisfied. God declares, "I will send it down to you."

With joy we invite our Muslim friends: come to the table. The feast is provided through the Messiah, who is the bread of life. He is the eternal feast who has come from heaven.

Miracles and appearances

An Ethiopian friend tells me of a time of hunger in his home region. He is a descendant of the original Muslim community that moved from Mecca to Ethiopia to acquire protection when the persecution of Muslims threatened to destroy the whole movement. So for 1,400 years his people have been bastions of the original Islam in Ethiopia.

My friend and his wife were hungry during a famine. They were prepared for the evening meal with just a little plate of macaroni. They would certainly go to bed hungry. Just then a neighbor appeared, and they needed to divide their inadequate meal into three portions. They ate, and continued eating, until all had adequate amounts. Ample macaroni still remained on the plate. All three looked under the table to see what was happening.

Then he remembered a Christian had told him Jesus had fed five thousand men miraculously by breaking five loaves of bread and two fish. They surmised their food multiplication had been a miracle wrought by the Messiah. So for the next two years he conducted his investigation. This consisted of observing the life and practices of the Christians. He was exceedingly impressed by their upright, loving, and humble lives. The miracle of multiplying macaroni was a necessary sign to put him on the way, but it was the actual Christian community that convinced him. He is now very involved in Ethiopia, sharing the good news of Jesus within Muslim communities; many have come to faith in the Messiah.

Appearances of the resurrected Messiah are often significant in opening doors for Muslims to consider Jesus. I asked a Catholic priest living in Khartoum what had been especially encouraging for him during his many years in Sudan. He said it was when the chief of a remote desert oasis town sent messengers to request that the priest come to meet with his village.

It was a lengthy journey. When the priest arrived, the chief explained, "A man appeared in the desert on the outer edges of our oasis village. The man was bright like the sun and he emanated pure love. I know he is the Messiah. He instructed me to send for you so that you can explain for me and the entire community the truths of God."

The priest described those wonderful days of meeting with an oasis village, introducing them to the Bible, Jesus, and the church. The community received the good news of the gospel with joy.

As I listen to accounts of the appearances of Jesus, they remind me of Saul in the book of Acts.[4] Saul was traveling from Jerusalem to Damascus, accompanied by soldiers in order to arrest Christians, whom he opposed passionately. On the road, the resurrected Jesus met him in brilliant glory. The risen Jesus instructed Saul to go to Damascus, where a disciple of Jesus would meet him and give him instructions.

---

4. Bible: Acts 9:1-19.

I frequently hear such accounts of Jesus the Messiah appearing and meeting Muslims. I believe these appearances are one way God is responding to the sincere faith of so many Muslims around the world. In these appearances the Messiah is brilliant light radiating perfect love. In the accounts, as in Saul's experience, the Messiah usually gives instruction to meet with a disciple of Jesus and learn more fully who he is. The appearance is a preparation for meeting a representative of the church. It seems God intends for these appearances to lead into fellowship and identification with the church. In some communities in Ethiopia, I am told, the appearances occasionally happen to imams who are positioned to lead their entire congregation of Muslims into faith in Jesus the Messiah.

Open doors: the church in Philadelphia

As we think of open doors, it is wise to consider the qualities that are needed for a person or community of believers in Jesus to engage with Muslims. The Lord's message to the church in Philadelphia is instructive. Jesus promises this church, "See, I have placed before you an open door that no one can shut."[5]

In chapter 2 we looked at the church in Philadelphia as a model of serving among Muslims with a clear identity (Revelation 3:7-13). Now we look at the same church to find five characteristics that are crucial for the door to open.

1. Practice brotherly and sisterly love

The Philadelphia church was in Asia Minor, which was thriving during the time of the biblical apostles. *Philadelphia* means "brotherly love." Doors open when we love others.

An example is the way Palestinian Christians have related to Hamas in Palestine. In the winter of 1992, Israel arrested 415 Hamas from Gaza and the West Bank and took them to a cold hillside in southern Lebanon. During the year of their detention, Palestinian and Lebanese Christians, with some assistance from churches abroad, met with the men detained on a hillside. They provided food, blankets, medicines, and letters and pictures from their families.[6]

---

5. Bible: Revelation 3:7.
6. Brother Andrew and Al Janssen, *Light Force: The Only Hope for the Middle East* (London: Hodder & Stoughton, 2004), 144–68.

When the men were finally released after a year, there was a great gathering in the mosque in Hebron to welcome the heroes home. Palestinian Christians wove their vehicle through the fields, avoiding roadblocks, until they arrived at the mosque. When the Hamas saw them, they addressed these Christians as their brothers who remembered them when the whole world had abandoned them. Thereafter, in several locations the Hamas invited the Palestinian Christians to distribute New Testaments in mosques and other venues. They knew it was Jesus who had inspired these Christians to serve so boldly in their extremity.

2. Do good deeds

The Palestinian Christians and their Lebanese partners expressed brotherly love to the Hamas. They also extended good deeds. I have mentioned conversations and dialogues my church community in North America has enjoyed with Iranian theologians, including my participation in the Mahdi conference. How did these doors open? The initial key opening the door was an airlift of blankets to Iran after an earthquake. The Iranians wondered who these Christians in North America were, who sent blankets in their time of need. Usually the good deeds are more low profile, like my wife preparing a dessert to welcome a Muslim family who moved next door to our home. Whether it is chartering airplanes with relief supplies or inviting a Muslim neighbor for a cup of coffee, good deeds open doors!

3. Rely on God's strength

It will surprise many that a third quality is little strength. When Christians approach Muslims in a spirit of strength, the walls will probably go up. In the world of geopolitical realities, that is most evident. The military strength of the United States, as exerted in the last few decades within the Muslim world, has not created trusting relations. In fact, some doors are closing tightly, even after hundreds of billions of dollars of military expenditure. A U.S. State Department officer told me she is jealous of the church, for we have open doors into countries and situations that have little or no relations with the United States. The way of Jesus the Messiah, who rode into Jerusalem on a colt, opens doors!

Those open doors are often surprising. In one of my visits to Iran, about a dozen of us North Americans were meeting with some Iranian theologians. At the end of our consultation, one of Iran's key spiritual leaders asked that I lead in prayer for peace between our nations. They addressed us as brothers.

4. Commit to the authority of the Bible

A fourth quality is commitment to the authority of the Scriptures. I have described the high regard the Qur'an has for the People of the Book, as well as recognizing the Bible as scripture.

When Kosovo was developing their constitution for an independent Kosovo, I was invited to speak to the Islamic department of a university on the theme of "Faith and Freedom." The writers of the constitution joined in the assembly. I positioned myself as a person of the Book and drew from the Torah and the Gospels in my presentation. The presentation was well received; I am most grateful that the Constitution of Kosovo as it was finally approved assures religious freedom for all citizens. I emphasize that other voices were also calling for religious freedom; however, I am told my presentation was heard and elicited much discussion. Why? Most certainly it was grounding the plea for religious freedom within the Scriptures that opened the door for serious debate and receptivity.

5. Do not deny Jesus

I have mentioned that Jesus the Messiah is the mystery figure of the Qur'an. There is curiosity about Jesus. Over the centuries Muslims have developed hundreds of poems and chants concerning Jesus. He is greatly loved. However, the Jesus of Muslim poetry is in conflict with the Jesus of the gospel. This is one key reason for the curiosity. Jesus is controversial.[7] Just consider the teachings of Jesus about how to relate to one's enemy. Can you imagine a more controversial teaching than the one Jesus interjects? *Love your enemy!* Talk about controversial ideas. There is an intrigue among many Muslims in regard to Jesus. It is difficult to have any conversation about faith with Muslims without Jesus occupying the center of the conversation.[8]

7. Tarif Khalidi, *The Muslim Jesus* (Cambridge, MA: Harvard University Press, 2001), 3–45.
8. Ibid., 44–45.

Some years ago I was teaching in the Baptist seminary in Sarajevo, Bosnia. I told the participants I would like to visit the Muslim center in the city. They were horrified and explained to me, "There has been a war between Orthodox Christians and Muslims in this city, and they will kill us." However, after some debate they surprised me by saying, "Rather than only you dying, we will all go with you and die together."

We introduced ourselves as a class at the Baptist seminary. Our Muslim hosts were thrilled. They said no Christian had ever before stopped by their center. They took us to the lounge and plied us with drinks and cookies as we plunged into heart-searching conversations. A couple of hours later, as we were leaving, they implored us to come again.

As we said our goodbyes, I asked, "Did you notice a Guest brought his chair into the circle as we gathered in the living room? In fact, he presided at our meeting."

"Yes," they acknowledged. "A Guest was present."

The Guest was Jesus. I am amazed at how consistently Jesus enters the circle when Muslims and Christians engage in conversations about faith. Neither Muslims nor Christians can easily ignore the presence of Jesus within our circle when we meet.

Enter the open doors

Fear is one of the primary reasons that Christians do not develop trusting relations with Muslims. Doors might be open, but we hesitate. That is what I experienced in Port Harcourt, Nigeria, recently. Our Christian/Muslim Relations Team had been invited to conduct a two-day seminar on peacemaking. In our acceptance letters to contribute to this gathering of some 350 leaders of Bible schools, we asked to meet with the Muslim leadership of this vast metropolis in southern Nigeria.

I arrived two days early and learned that, in light of recent attacks against churches in northwestern Nigeria, the sponsors of the seminar thought it would not be wise to meet Muslim leaders at that time. We asked, "How can one have a seminar on Christian-Muslim relations and meet no Muslims?" We all committed the matter to prayer.

Toward the end of the seminar, a relative of the grand imam of Port Harcourt spoke to the imam, who agreed to meet with representatives of these Christians leaders. Participants in the seminar were astonished and elated. Five Christian leaders and five Muslims met for one hour. At the beginning of the meeting, our team member confessed that the reason for his persistence in peacemaking is that Jesus was crucified and is risen.

The imam objected. "Christ was never crucified," he insisted. Much of the hour was then invested in dialogue about the meaning of the cross in Christian experience. At the end of the meeting, the imam requested that the Christians keep in contact and plan for other substantive conversations.

After that, those who had come for the seminar scattered. One of the pastors at the seminar met some Muslim university students in his home city. In the past he had mistrusted Muslim students. This time, however, he told them boldly that he had just concluded a seminar on Christian-Muslim relations. The students were captivated, and they asked the pastor to meet with them regularly to teach them what he had learned at the seminar.

Our calling as emissaries of the Messiah is to find doors through the walls. Often Jesus and the ministries of the church have already opened the door, but we think it is closed. We need to listen! We need to knock. We need to discern. It is Jesus who goes before us, unlocking the doors. As we flow in prayer, the Holy Spirit goes before us showing the way, revealing the doors Jesus has opened. The calling of ambassadors of Christ is just this: to prayerfully discern where the doors are opening and to enter those doors as Christ's emissaries.

Recently I received a phone call from a happy man. He said, "David, I was traveling with my Muslim neighbor to town and asked if he would have interest in meeting with me for a study of the Bible. He was delighted I would take time to meet with him. We are anticipating our first Bible study. We are going to explore the biblical narrative together."

The surprise of church

The creation of the church in any society is a miracle. I have witnessed the miracle of church again and again as I participate in

Muslim countries and societies around the world. Church in its most foundational meaning is when two or more meet and worship together in the name of Jesus the Messiah. The worldwide church consists of several million local congregations where this happens.

For example, I am a member of a local congregation in the village of Mountville in the United States. I am also a member of the worldwide church. In chapter 5 we looked at the church as the new city God is creating, a community comprising people from every language and nation. We discover that Jesus, crucified and risen, is standing in the center of the church, both the local church and the universal church. I will describe one example of the church—namely, the Somali-speaking church in Nairobi, Kenya, where Ahmed and his family were members.

At that time, there were two major ways Somalis became believers in Jesus the Messiah. First was the ministry to Somali refugees that Ahmed and his family were deeply engaged in. Then there was the availability of the Bible and a study course about the Bible written especially for Muslims (*People of God*, the course I mentioned in chapter 4).

Whenever I got to Nairobi, I would do my best to go to this church that met under Ahmed's tree. Sometimes as many as eighty people met, most of them widows from the Somali wars and their children. Sometimes Ahmed would lead in the singing, with children using a table as their drum. They sang in praise to God for Jesus the Messiah, in whom they had found salvation and hope. The tunes and lyrics were mostly developed by Somali believers. The gathering was also a time for sharing their stories, praying, and hearing preaching based on the Bible.

Ahmed told me of one amazing gathering for reconciliation. Somalia was in turmoil, largely because of conflict between clans. So the elders of the Somali church encouraged leaders from clans across the Somali world to meet for a reconciliation event. Ahmed told me all the Somali clans were represented. They prayed and listened to the preaching of the Word of God, then began to confess their sins of interclan hatred. Some wept as they asked forgiveness. "That day," Ahmed told me, "heaven came to earth!"

The church concluded this miraculous gathering with a communion service. They took bread and fruit drink and shared with one another, as they remembered the body of Jesus the Messiah, broken on the cross like the kernels of grain were broken. They drank from the cup, remembering the blood of Jesus poured out on the hill where he was crucified. This gathering of the church in reconciliation was a precious event.

Ahmed exclaimed, "It was a miracle!"

A message from Cairo

Indeed, there are many signs of hope! When in Cairo in June 2013, I met the assistant to the Grand Mufti of Egypt, the highest official of religious law, in his office in Al-Azhar University. I told him I am a Christian who yearns to walk in the peace of the Messiah and bear witness to his peace. I explained that I participate in the fellowship of the church wherever I go. I invest my ministry especially in peacemaking between Muslims and Christians. I encourage people to embrace the peace of the Messiah, in whom there is healing and new life.

The Grand Mufti's assistant responded by saying that he hoped I could come to Cairo again before too long and that he would try to arrange for me to give a public lecture at the university on the peace of Jesus.

When I asked him what message he has for North American Christians, he said, "I have two words of advice. First, it would be helpful for the churches in North America to really work with Middle East Christians toward an Israeli-Palestinian peace accord. We feel that North American Christians are in a position where they could actively encourage movements toward justice and peace. My second word of advice is that North Americans need to follow Jesus. For if they followed Jesus, they would become part of a life-giving transformation movement throughout the whole world."

Here I was, meeting a top Muslim leader in Egypt, and he was commending Christ to North American Christians!

Living in hope

Most Muslims are eager to converse about God. My observation is that, of all religious people, Muslims are the most ready to discuss and debate faith. God-awareness permeates Muslim societies. In the most mundane conversations, God-awareness weaves into the speech.

For example, I cannot imagine a Muslim saying, "I will meet you at the car in five minutes." Rather a Muslim would say, "I will meet at the car in five minutes, *Inshallah* (God willing)." Muslims appreciate when Christians also demonstrate awareness of God. The God-awareness of Muslims is usually an open door for conversations about faith.

Cultivating commitments to the twelve paths for relationship-building with Muslims does not require being an expert. But it does require prayerfully entering the doors God is opening.

A pastor from a restrictive country in central Asia told me, "I always feared the imam in the mosque on a hill overlooking my town. I thought of him as my enemy. I prayed about my fears. Then one day I decided to take steps to change our relationship. I climbed the hill to the imam's home. I met him, and we had tea together. After that I went back to his home on the hill again and again. I began to consult with him about our church. He became my advocate. I even told him about baptisms I was planning. When the Muslim villagers objected, the imam told them that I had consulted with him, and the baptisms were just fine."

We appreciate such accounts of peacemaking. Yet it is not always that way. Sometimes, no matter how we seek to develop real Christian-Muslim relationship, the reciprocity is not there. Especially in recent years, the global political situation has sometimes fueled hatred or fear which can get out of control. I am writing this chapter in June 2014. This has been a horrendous month of mayhem and destruction, from Syria to Nigeria. Horrible violence has been wrought in the name of God! The church is present within all these regions of strife.

Paradoxically, I have experienced hope this week. I spoke by phone with a church leader in central Nigeria, where there have been terrorist attacks. I will be visiting him shortly. He said, "This is a good time for you to come. Praise the Lord! There are many open doors for peacemaking. These are remarkable days of opportunity to serve Jesus as an emissary of his peace."

The church has special responsibilities for peacemaking, for it is present within all these areas of conflict. We know that in the Messiah there is reconciliation. Paul writes, "Therefore, my dear brothers and sisters, stand firm. Let nothing move you. Always give yourselves fully to the work of the Lord, because you know that your labor in the Lord is not in vain."[9]

So we live with integrity. We keep our identity clear. We cultivate respect. We develop trust. We dialogue about our differences. We practice hospitality. We answer the questions. We confront the distortions. We consider the choice between the *hijrah* and the cross. We seek peace and pursue it. We partner with the person of peace. We commend Christ.

And as we walk down these paths, we live in hope.

Questions for discussion

1. Comment on the five qualities Jesus highlights in regard to the church in Philadelphia.

2. In what ways do these qualities equip Christians for engagement with Muslims? Give some examples of the door being opened for Christians to engage Muslims and become their friends.

3. Consider reasons that Muslims have so much interest in conversations about God. What surprises might Jesus offer in those conversations?

4. Do you have a friendship with a Muslim? If so, describe the friendship. If you do not have a Muslim friend, consider ways a friendship might develop.

5. How would you commend the gospel to a Muslim acquaintance?

6. What do you especially appreciate about Muslims?

7. Review all twelve paths. Which of these paths are gifts you bring to the table in developing real relationship with Muslims?

---

9. Bible: 1 Corinthians 15:58.

APPENDIX A
Christian/Muslim Relations Team

Author's note: I am a participant in a modest global network of believers in Jesus the Messiah who are seeking to serve as peacemakers in the way of Christ among Christians and Muslims. Below are our commitments as peacemakers confessing Christ.

But in your hearts revere Christ as Lord.
Always be prepared to give an answer to everyone
who asks you to give the reason for the hope that
you have. But do this with gentleness and respect.
—1 Peter 3:15

Our witness-bearing commitment
In obedience to Jesus' command to be witnesses among all nations (Matthew 28:18-20) and to the apostolic exhortation to commend Christ with gentleness and respect (1 Peter 3:8-17), we bear witness to the good news of salvation, forgiveness, redemption, and reconciliation that God offers in Jesus the Messiah. We seek to do so in ways that are both faithful to Christ and sincerely respectful of each person's dignity, culture, and freedom of choice.

We desire to share in ways that are faithful to the following commitments:

1. To reflect and honor the spirit and values of the Messiah.
2. To be true to the gospel as revealed in the biblical Scriptures.
3. To communicate God's deep love for all.
4. To depend on God's Holy Spirit to reveal truth and transform lives.
5. To reject the use of all forms of violence, imperialism, bribery, intimidation, coercion, vilification, misrepresentation, and deceit.
6. To pursue peace, dialogue, and mutual understanding.
7. To listen and respond carefully to the questions, objections, and witness others may have for us.
8. To be honest and sincere and willing to suffer for the sake of justice and the truth.
9. To be respectful of people of other cultures, languages, and faiths.
10. To be ready to sacrifice for the well-being of our fellow humans.
11. To seek to build up the local and worldwide church, the body of Christ.
12. To take seriously the unique value of each person, language, and culture.
13. To respect the governing authorities.
14. To hold parents, children, and family life in high esteem.
15. To fully recognize each person's dignity and freedom of choice.

Names and Characteristics of Jesus in the Qur'an

Author's note: This is a limited selection of Qur'anic references to Jesus. There are references to Jesus in "the Traditions" that I have not mentioned. Muslim poetry and narrative also contain many allusions to Jesus. It is evident that we need to tread cautiously when reviewing the references to Jesus in just this one source: the Qur'an. Each statement needs to be understood in the context of the total understanding of Jesus, not just selective references. Having said that, it is appropriate to begin here and ask the question: what does the Qur'an say about Jesus?

- Isa is his name. (The Arabic *Yasua*, meaning "Yahweh saves," is not used.)
- Jesus is like Adam (3:59).
- Jesus is a sign (43:61-64).
- Jesus is the Messiah (3:45).
- Jesus is the Word of God (4:171).
- Jesus is the Spirit of God (4:41).
- Jesus was born of the virgin (Miriam, sister of Moses) (19:16-35).
- Jesus was a miracle worker (3:49).
- Jesus established the former scriptures (5:49).
- Jesus brought the gospel (5:49).
- Jesus is only an apostle (6:71).

- Jesus was rescued from the cross and another takes his place; this means that Jesus was not crucified (4:157).
- Jesus was taken to heaven without dying (3:55-58).
- Jesus will return to earth again at the conclusion of history to prepare the world for the final judgment by turning people toward Islam (43:61).
- Jesus was sent to Israel for a specific time and mission (13:38).
- Jesus is not the Son of God (9:30).
- Jesus fulfills the former scriptures (5:49).
- The Messiah is good news (3:45).
- Jesus predicted the coming of Muhammad (61:6).
- Jesus is sinless (19:19).

In its most simple form, the Muslim worldview is formed by the *Ikhlas*: the Purity of Faith. The Muslim understanding of Jesus is formed by this passage:

> In the name of God, Most gracious, Most Merciful
> Say, he is God the One and only.
> God the eternal absolute
> He begetteth not, nor is he begotten
> And there is none Like unto Him.[1]

---

1. Qur'an: *Ikhlas* (the Purity of Faith): surah 112:1-4.

APPENDIX C

References to the Bible in the Qur'an

Author's note: This is a sampling of Qur'anic verses that make reference to the biblical Scriptures. This list was developed for the book *Journeys of the Muslim Nation and the Christian Church* and are organized here into two major themes.

1. God has revealed former scriptures.

- He [Allah] sent down the Law [*Taurat* of the Prophet Moses], and the Gospel [*Injil* of Jesus the Messiah] (*Ali Imran* 3:3).
- For to them was entrusted the protection of God's Book (*Maida* 5:47).
- People of the Book, you have no ground to stand upon unless you stand fast by the Law [*Taurat*] and the Gospel [*Injil*] and all the revelation that has come to you from your Lord (*Maida* 5:68).
- The writings of Moses are the *furqan* of truth (*Anbiyaa* 21:48 and *Baqara* 2:53).
- It is also guidance, light, and mercy to humankind. It is the Book of Allah (*Maida* 5:44; *Hud* 11:17; *Anibiyaa* 21:48).
- No change can there be in the Words of God (*Yunus* 10:64).

- *In regard to the gospel, the Qur'an states:* Therein was guidance and light and confirmation of the law [*Taurat*] had come before him [the Messiah] a guidance and an admonition (*Maida* 5:49).
- *The Qur'an also advises the Prophet Muhammad:* If thou wert in doubt as to what we have revealed unto thee, then ask those who have been reading the Book from before thee (*Yunus* 10:94).
- *Occasionally the Qur'an insists God's Word cannot be corrupted. Here is an example of this kind of affirmation:* Rejected were the Apostles before thee; with patience and constancy they bore their rejection and their wrongs, until our aid did reach them; there is none that can alter the Words and Decrees of God (*Anam* 6:34).

2. The People of the Book must respect and protect their Scriptures.

There are also admonitions for the Christians not to corrupt their Scriptures, not to hide their Scriptures or sell Scripture for a profit, and not to misquote the Scripture.

- And remember, God took a Covenant from the People of the Book, to make it known and clear to mankind, and not to hide it (*Ali Imran* 3:187).
- There is among them a section that distorts the Book with their tongues; [as they read] you would think it is part of the Book, but it is not part of the Book, and they say, "it is from God," but it is not from God; it is they who tell a lie against God, and well they know it (*Ali Imran* 3:78).
- Ye People of the Book! Why do ye clothe with falsehood, and conceal the Truth, while ye have knowledge (*Ali Imran* 3:71).
- Then woe to those who write the Book with their own hands, and then say: "This is from God," to traffic with it for a miserable price!—Woe to them for what their hands do write and for the gain they make thereby (*Baqara* 2:79).

APPENDIX D

A Mennonite Response to "A Common Word"

Author's note: Below is a Mennonite response to a letter from Muslim leaders sent to Christians around the world. Originally signed by 138 Muslim clerics, "A Common Word between Us and You" garnered a variety of responses from Christian groups. (The full text of the letter is available at the letter's official website: www.acommonword.com.) I often refer to this 2007 response from the Mennonites as a good example of the paths of respect, dialogue about differences, and the pursuit of peace.

To the Muslim Religious Leaders who signed the October 13, 2007, letter, "A Common Word between Us and You," addressed to Leaders of Christian churches throughout the world:

As one of the historic peace churches, we in Mennonite Church USA heartily thank the signatories of "A Common Word Between Us and You" for recognizing that Christians worship one God and take Jesus' commands to love God and love our neighbors as central to our lives of faith. We appreciate the affirmation that Muslims and Christians hold important theological and ethical foundations in common, and we welcome the call for sincere dialogue between Christians and Muslims wherever we meet around the world.

We also respect "A Common Word" as a courageous expression of goodwill in the midst of less charitable Muslim voices and in the face of recurrent Christian hostility toward Muslims and misunderstanding of Islam. We repent for our role in perpetrating these unchristian actions and ask your patience and forgiveness as we grow in understanding you, our Muslim neighbors, and in practicing Christian love with you.

We understand the character of this love to be shaped by the teaching and personal example of Jesus. In addition to loving God and our neighbors, this means that we aim to love even enemies and, like Jesus, we choose against using violence as a response to difference and conflict. We believe that Jesus has modeled for us a life of faithful obedience to God based on love, truth, reconciliation, and justice. We seek the same, in response to God's love for all humankind expressed in innumerable acts of salvation, reconciliation, forgiveness and guidance, and most fully in Jesus Christ (the Messiah). In sum, "We love because he first loved us" (1 John 4:19). In our faltering attempts to love as the Messiah loved, we thank God for the gift of his Spirit who enables us to live our lives focused on God.

God has given each person the precious gift of choice, even the freedom to believe in God or turn to unbelief. In our Mennonite churches, adult baptism is a sign of the individual's decision to believe in and follow the Messiah. For that reason we baptize only after a person has made a mature decision to believe and to turn away from the ways of the world.

Our life as a church thereby witnesses to society and government, that each person has the responsibility and freedom to choose their faith. We believe that in any society, the love of neighbor that you have so eloquently written about includes respect for that person's freedom to believe or not to believe, to choose his or her faith and religion. We would indeed welcome opportunity to talk more with Muslim friends and leaders about the implications of religious freedom for this matter that is of profound significance.

With you, we embrace the goal of loving our neighbors, while also recognizing that both Muslims and Christians often fall short of the ideal. We recognize that even today in too many situations Muslims are threatened by Christians, and in other situations, individual Christians or communities of Christians in

Muslim regions experience restrictions and sometimes hostility. Let us repent of such actions toward one another and work together to assure the integrity and freedom for both communities, Christian and Muslim.

Many Mennonite Christians have enjoyed friendship with Muslims and cooperated together in a wide range of activities through the years. We in Mennonite Church USA continue to commend such interaction and strongly encourage Christians and Muslims around the world to meet, develop friendships, and cooperate in endeavors of mutual concern as we discuss and bear witness to the theological and ethical foundations of our faith and life.

We thank those who have issued "A Common Word," and assure you that we will continue to pray and work for Christian-Muslim understanding, cooperation, and peacemaking.

Sincerely,

—James Schrag
Executive Director, Mennonite Church USA

APPENDIX E

Shared Convictions of Anabaptists

Author's note: This list of seven shared convictions was adopted by the global body of Anabaptists in 2006. It offers a window into the theology and witness of Anabaptism.

By the grace of God, we seek to live and proclaim the good news of reconciliation in Jesus Christ. As part of the one body of Christ at all times and places, we hold the following to be central to our belief and practice:

1. God is known to us as Father, Son, and Holy Spirit, the Creator who seeks to restore fallen humanity by calling a people to be faithful in fellowship, worship, service, and witness.
2. Jesus is the Son of God. Through his life and teachings, his cross and resurrection, he showed us how to be faithful disciples, redeemed the world, and offers eternal life.
3. As a church, we are a community of those whom God's Spirit calls to turn from sin, acknowledge Jesus Christ as Lord, receive baptism upon confession of faith, and follow Christ in life.
4. As a faith community, we accept the Bible as our authority for faith and life, interpreting it together under Holy Spirit guidance, in the light of Jesus Christ to discern God's will for our obedience.

5. The Spirit of Jesus empowers us to trust God in all areas of life so we become peacemakers who renounce violence, love our enemies, seek justice, and share our possessions with those in need.

6. We gather regularly to worship, to celebrate the Lord's Supper, and to hear the Word of God in a spirit of mutual accountability.

7. As a worldwide community of faith and life we transcend boundaries of nationality, race, class, gender, and language. We seek to live in the world without conforming to the powers of evil, witnessing to God's grace by serving others, caring for creation, and inviting all people to know Jesus Christ as Savior and Lord.

In these convictions we draw inspiration from Anabaptist forebears of the sixteenth century, who modeled radical discipleship to Jesus Christ. We seek to walk in his name by the power of the Holy Spirit, as we confidently await Christ's return and the final fulfillment of God's kingdom.

Adopted by Mennonite World Conference
General Council
March 15, 2006

The Author

David W. Shenk is global consultant
for Eastern Mennonite Missions.
Author or coauthor of fifteen books
and several booklets, including *A
Muslim and a Christian in Dialogue,
Journeys of the Muslim Nation and
the Christian Church,* and *Teatime
in Mogadishu,* Shenk visits about fifteen countries a year, engaging in dialogues or serving as a lecturer in both
Christian and Muslim forums.

Shenk holds a doctorate in reli-
gious studies education from New York University, with course-
work in anthropology. He and his wife, Grace, have four children
and seven grandchildren. They live in Mountville, Pennsylvania.

Read all the books in the
Christians Meeting Muslims series from Herald Press

DIALOGUE

A Muslim and a Christian in Dialogue, 2nd ed.
Badru D. Kateregga and David W. Shenk
978-0-8361-9619-1, $14.99 USD

Listen in on the conversation between a devout Muslim and a devout Christian as they confess their faith to one another. In this distinctive book, two friends address basic questions of the human situation and confront areas of convergence and divergence between Islam and Christianity. Muslim-Christian interactions are at times antagonistic. Here Badru D. Kateregga and David W. Shenk pioneer another way: that of authentic and respectful dialogue.

WITNESS AND INVITATION

Journeys of the Muslim Nation and the Christian Church:
Exploring the Mission of Two Communities
David W. Shenk
978-0-8361-9252-0, $14.99 USD

Most Muslims have questions about the Christian faith; are you prepared to respond? Is the Bible trustworthy? Why do you believe in three gods? How can you say that Jesus the Messiah is God's son? What do you think of Muhammad? How is it possible for the Messiah to be crucified? This book will equip Christians to respond with gentle boldness and respect to questions about their faith.

PEACEMAKING

Teatime in Mogadishu
My Journey as a Peace Ambassador in the World of Islam
Ahmed Ali Haile, as told to David W. Shenk
978-0-8361-9557-6, $14.99 USD

A tireless ambassador for Christ, Ahmed Ali Haile returned to the chaos of his native Somalia with a clear mission: to bring warring clans together to find new paths of peace, often over a cup of tea. A grenade thrown by a detractor cost Haile his leg and almost his life, but his stature as a peacemaker remained. Learn of Haile's bold faith and his joy in suffering for the love of his own people and his love for Jesus his Lord.

FRIENDSHIP

Christian. Muslim. Friend.
Twelve Paths to Real Relationship
David W. Shenk
978-0-8361-9905-5, $14.99 USD

Can Christians and Muslims be friends? Real friends? Even in an era of intense religious conflict, David W. Shenk says yes. Shenk lays out twelve ways that Christians can form authentic relationships with Muslims—characterized by respect, hospitality, and candid dialogue—while still speaking clearly about Jesus.

**Order any of these books at 1-800-245-7894 (US) /
1-800-631-6535 (Canada) or from www.heraldpress.com.**

CPSIA information can be obtained
at www.ICGtesting.com
Printed in the USA
LVOW01s1037170116
471044LV00020B/1092/P